ayun halliday

dirty Sugar Cookies

culinary observations, questionable taste

SEAL PRESS

for mom, gran, and inky

Published by Seal Press
An Imprint of Avalon Publishing Group, Incorporated
1400 65th Street, Suite 250
Emeryville, CA 94608

ISBN-13: 978-1-58005-150-7
ISBN-10: 1-58005-150-2

9 8 7 6 5 4 3 2 1

Library of Congress Cataloging-in-Publication Data

Halliday, Ayun.
Dirty sugar cookies : culinary observations, questionable taste / Ayun Halliday.
p. cm.
ISBN-13: 978-1-58005-150-7
ISBN-10: 1-58005-150-2
1. Cookery. 2. Cookery—Humor. 3. Gastronomy—Humor. I. Title.
TX652.H345 2006
641.502'07—dc22
2005037671

Book design by Kate Basart / Union Pageworks
Printed in the United States of America by Malloy
Distributed by Publishers Group West

contents

au jus

I wasn't born this omnivorous, this game to devour ant eggs on sticky rice, barbequed eel, chipotle peppers in adobo sauce, fresh durian, reeking cheese rimed in mold, or a peanut M&M discovered wedged in the crack of a theater seat's cushion. In my youth I was picky, just like my eight-year-old daughter, whose ongoing lack of culinary adventurousness drives me right out of my fucking gourd. Of course, even the strictest pickiness has its loopholes. I suspect that Inky, and, for that matter, the child me, would prioritize good luck over modern hygiene as regards that peanut M&M, which, by the way, was a real M&M, not some hypothetical metaphor cooked up to show you what a good eater I've become. I forget what color it was, but when I happened upon it in Chicago's Music Box Theater sometime in the early '90s, I did not hesitate. I take my manna where I find it, then as now.

I should also stress that when I say "omnivorous," what I mean is everything excepting poultry and red meat, a self-imposed dietary restriction that most of the people I knew growing up would consider both vegetarian and bizarre to the point of sashimi.

"Does Indiana have a signature dish?" a friend who was born and reared in New York City inquired as we were tucking into some chopped liver from Barney Greengrass shortly after I moved here, a decade ago now. I must have looked at him blankly. "You know, like Philly cheesesteak or gumbo or schmaltz?"

"Uh . . . I guess maybe corn."

"Corn!" he exploded. "They've got corn in New Jersey! Every farmers market from Union Square to my ass has corn. I'm talking something special, something every tourist has to eat at least once. Corn."

"Okay, well, in that case, maybe funnel cakes. They're like elephant ears poured through a funnel. You get them at the state fair." My friend started to shake his head. These native New Yorkers think they're so big, always trying to remind us of our place relative to theirs. "They're not unlike beignets," I lied unconvincingly. I knew all about those, growing up in Indiana, but only because my French teacher told me.

Would I have been any less picky if I'd been exposed to the culinary advantages my friend took for granted, having spent his entire childhood in New York City, where even the hot dog stand boasted such exotica as papaya juice and coconut champagne? Probably not, though of course I like to think so. Growing up, I didn't dine out all that much and when I did, the menu tended to reflect the kinds of things I was served at home. My mother and grandmother were both excellent home cooks, not that I deigned to eat much of their output.

My grandmother, who lived just around the corner from us in a densely settled part of Indianapolis, cooked as if she expected a crowd of hungry farmhands to turn up for the noon meal instead of just Grampy and me. As soon as she put the breakfast dishes away, Gran would haul out a big tub of Crisco and her three-legged electric skillet and start frying up some chicken. Biscuits, stewed apples, mashed potatoes, corn on the cob, Jell-O salad, spinach (I think it came from a can—I never touched it), iced tea, and chocolate cake—basically, it was the same fare that Mama's Food Shop, an East Village stalwart renowned for its campy thrift store décor and its flaming staff, dishes up with a side of irony. My friend Little MoMo, who grew up in Orange County, couldn't get enough of this trendy, all-American comfort food, though Lord knows she tried, befriending a waiter who routinely loaded her up with shopping bags full of unsold leftovers when Mama's closed for the night. "Ooh, I'm going to fuck me up some of these baked beans," she'd promise, whipping the top off an aluminum foil takeout container. "Better grab some if you want some, because when I'm done, there ain't gonna be any left for the grabbing."

Funny, my grandmother used to push baked beans on me too, albeit in slightly different vocabulary. The only time Gran said "ain't" was when it slipped out unconsciously.

"No, you take them all," I'd tell my friend. "I've been fixating on that Homestyle Bean Curd from Viet Café. I may just dart around the corner for a second and get some of that." Now, there's a fine example of something one would never, ever say or hear in 1970s Indianapolis. No matter what the Thanksgiving issue of *Gourmet* would have us believe, comfort food is not always what one grew up eating or, more accurately, refusing to eat.

My mother, who as a bride had worked her way through Julia Child's *Mastering the Art of French Cooking* dish by dish, was more of a gourmet and thus more of a problem for a child whose sense of culinary adventure was as pinched as mine. I've blotted out the specifics of the dishes she labored over for hours, they were so traumatic. I liked her desserts just fine, but nearly everything else induced a cringe. Dinnertime was a trial, though I took great pride in our grandly appointed formal dining room. It had red flocked wallpaper, a crystal chandelier, and large windows through which my parents occasionally claimed to spot an elf gathering evidence for Santa of my goodness or lack thereof. Unfortunately, my mother, who left a career in journalism to stay at home and raise her only child, had all the time in the world to reduce sauces and braise shallots, ensuring that every evening meal would match the elegance of the room in which it was served. My love of fanciness stopped at the plate, in those days a gold-rimmed minefield of tomato aspic, intentionally wilted salads, and expensive meats served au jus.

"Isn't it wonderful your mother's such a talented cook?" glamorous guests in tastefully modest beehives and pearls demanded at the dinner parties I was considered well mannered enough to attend. A feature on her that ran in the *Indianapolis Star*'s "Seasoning and Savoring" column on May 17, 1970, opened, "Mrs. Reed E. Halliday doesn't condemn casseroles though she thinks men prefer steak or roasts as main dishes," and went on to share her recipes for Spinach Mornay, Far East Celery, and Brandied Blue Cheese Spread. It matters little that these preparations now strike me as wholly reasonable, if a bit unnecessarily heavy on the saturated fats; as an only child, I was held prisoner to them. I had no older siblings to spirit me off to the local pizza parlor, and no younger siblings to exhaust the chef into cracking open a can of SpaghettiOs. The only time I got Burger Chef was on special occasions, like when a baby sitter was coming or my pet cat had been euthanized, but even then we had to bring it home to eat off real china. Even with tears running into my mouth over the fate of poor Simpkin, those fries tasted so good—probably because they were crisped in butcher's refuse by somebody who didn't give a damn whether I ate them or not.

Not that tofu, tuna belly, and turmeric could be procured at Atlas Supermarket, back when my Hoosier homeboy David Letterman was bagging groceries, but I wonder what would have happened if the woman I grew up to be could have had a hand in feeding the child I was then. That'd be a juicy matter to take up with the psychiatrist, if only I had one. I probably should, given Inky's tearful reaction to the hair-raising cuisine issuing from her mother's kitchen. When I was a kid, I couldn't believe that the starving Africans I was periodically shamed into thinking about would feel gratitude had they, by some miracle, gotten a crack at the jellied bouillon my mother placed before me on an equally horrifying lettuce leaf. Now I find it difficult to believe that my daughter, who is so compassionate and interested in other cultures, actively despises fish tacos, especially when there are children in Darfur who'd jump through hoops for just one bite. How can she hate hummus and Buddha's Delight and the awe-inspiring five-dollar ceviche from the food stands that materialize next to the Red Hook pool every warm-weather weekend? "You said these would taste like brownies," she says, rejecting a plate of mochi drizzled with rice syrup after a reluctant exploratory nibble.

Ah, hubris. "You don't know what you're missing!" I insist, nullifying my morning workout by devouring the treat I claimed to have purchased specially for her.

"You're just saying that because you love everything," she counters.

So help me, it's true. Except pasta, which I hate. And meat, which I confess I still harbor very tender feelings for, as if it were someone I was in love with long ago. Sometimes I tarry at *souvlaki* carts just to smell. "One day, you'll love everything too," I tell my daughter, who receives this prophecy with an expression of extreme dubiousness. I pop another mochi in my mouth, even though it's not really cool enough to eat and the remains of the one that immediately preceded it have welded onto my molars. "Trust me, I know. You can't stay picky forever."

spinach mornay

"Betsy Halliday reduces the "secret" of being a good cook to an uncompromising demand that all ingredients be fresh and high quality. In fact, she would prefer shopping daily for fresh foods but admits that the schedule of the 1970 housewife hardly permits this."

—Verna McCallum, food editor, the Indianapolis Star, *Sunday, May 17, 1970*

Cook 3 10-oz packages of frozen chopped spinach using no additional water. I guess this is what constituted "fresh" in 1970, but I might suggest interpreting freshness according to the twenty-first-century definition, by briefly steaming 3 or, hell, 4 never-been-frozen bunches.

Melt 4 tablespoons of butter, remove from heat, then add:

3 tablespoons of flour
1½ teaspoon of Dijon mustard
1 teaspoon of mustard powder
a pinch of cayenne
salt to taste

Whisk in 1 cup of milk, bring the mixture to a boil, then add 3 tablespoons of grated swiss, ¼ cup of grated parmesan, and 4 tablespoons of cream.

Simmer for five minutes, then combine with spinach. No word on what sort of dish you're supposed to use, but as I recall, the 1970s housewife didn't lack for festive casseroles. Whatever you choose, you're free to throw it in the fridge for a few hours while you run to the beauty parlor, or perhaps to Lafayette Square to pick up that 10-gallon shop vacuum that's advertised in the *Star* for a mere $19.99. Not bad for a permanently lubricated ball bearing motor and a triangular utility nozzle.

Bake in a 350° oven for 15 minutes. Grate some (fresh!) parmesan atop, then bake for 5 minutes more.

fruit basket upset

In addition to her sequined tap-dancing costumes and the pink ostrich-plume pen she refused to share when we played school, Darla Kratt got to have the Enchanted Castle Cake from Betty Crocker's *New Boys and Girls Cookbook*. Seeing that thing displayed beneath the Kratts' chandelier at Darla's eighth birthday party filled me with such spite, I could have taken the Holly Hobbie doll I was to give her and rammed it down her throat.

Situated on a vast lawn of shredded coconut dyed green, the Enchanted Castle boasted ice-cream-cone turrets and ramparts made of pillow mints. Hershey bar sections were embedded in the frosting like a drawbridge and windows. It was a dead ringer for the photograph on page 101, but better, since Mrs. Kratt had taken the liberty of adding some small plastic knights belonging to Darla's younger brother, Crazy Craig. Not even the miniature bottles of pastel nail polish set out as party favors next to each guest's nut cup could divert me from the inequity of this grail's being bestowed upon someone who already had everything: big-eyed Walter Keane paintings, a patio umbrella, one of those dolls whose voluminous crocheted skirts concealed an extra roll of toilet paper. I moped until Crazy Craig swiped one of the turrets, a breach of security that predictably caused the birthday girl to flee in tears. Now that was a spirit-lifter.

After a brief interval during which Craig was punished, Darla was consoled, and the rest of us nearly came to blows over who had been dealt the best color of nail polish, the cake was doled out onto princess-themed paper plates. All it took was one mouthful for the Enchanted Castle to wholly disenchant. I couldn't believe it. The white "walls" hummed with a chemical sweetness to rival that of those frosting roses we battled each other for under more standard refreshment circumstances. Having kept my fingers crossed for devil's food, I experienced something like vertigo when the interior was revealed to be a decidedly nonchocolate shade of pale. The only nonchocolate cake I considered worthy was Gran-Gran's angel food, cloaked in pink boiled icing and festooned with the bird-shaped pink and blue plastic candle-holders she broke out for family birthdays.

Please let there be ice cream, I bowed my head to pray. *Even if it's orange sherbet.* Nearly eight years old myself, I had amassed enough experience with other kids' birthdays to know that a cake's beauty is, more often than not, inversely proportional to its flavor. I'd always assumed this was because other kids had store-bought cakes that, to my dismay, seemed but rarely available in chocolate. Even before I could read, I knew enough to mistrust those large rectangular jobbies iced with personalized birthday greetings and semiaccurate portraits of cartoon characters.

I remember one that got the mothers oohing and ahhing as they escorted us into the skating rink for a classmate's party. This was clearly the expected reaction, since the hostess made a point of steering them past the bench where her daughter's cake lay in state in its white cardboard box. A puddle of gelatinous turquoise goo had been professionally poured atop its vast, shortening-rich expanse and a plastic figure skater positioned mid-arabesque near its edge, creating the illusion that the gliding motion of her supporting foot had etched the elaborate turquoise-on-white HAPPY BIRTHDAY FELICIA. It was gaudy, glamorous, thematic—everything a schoolgirl could desire, except that it also tasted like Crisco by way of cough syrup. The cakes my mother and grandmother baked for me tasted like actual ingredients, the ones I tried to sneak out of the kitchen cabinet when they weren't looking.

Given a blind taste test, I would have sworn that Darla's Enchanted Castle had come from Rosy Roslyn's, the brightly lit local institution responsible for previous years' ballerina- and circus-themed monstrosities. I couldn't have begun to speculate what such a gorgeous specimen would have run Darla's parents in a bakery. Five hundred dollars, maybe, a price only a movie star could afford. I had never imagined that I would actually see the Enchanted Castle in the flesh, that anyone's mother would embark upon such a structurally complex confection, that green coconut grass could be found outside the pages of Betty Crocker's *New Boys and Girls Cookbook*. Every girl at Darla's table owned that book; we all understood the significance of Mrs. Kratt's having cooked the most impossibly special thing in it. Its photograph was so magical that even after Darla's party, I continued to think *I'll bet that tastes wonderful* every time I turned to page 101 in my personal copy, given to me by my grandparents in honor of my sixth birthday. Even though I was a precocious reader, it took me a couple of years to decipher Gran's wobbly cursive well enough to make out the inscription:

Happy Cooking, Anne! You can make your mother, Daddy, and Friends lots of goodies. —Much Love, Your Gran & Grampy, 1971.

Reading that anachronistic inscription is a bittersweet experience for me now, though I suppose it'll go a long way toward clearing up the controversy surrounding the pronunciation of my first name. For one thing, my grandmother didn't live to see the publication of my first book, let alone this one whose title she inspired. (It's okay. The language alone would have fucking killed her.) Also, it's been nearly thirty years since my parents shared a meal, unless one counts the hors d'oeuvres passed on trays at my wedding, which my generally easygoing father condemned as "mostly crackers."

Like he's got room to talk! The man's culinary repertoire is limited to two dishes, a paprika-sprinkled baked chicken breast thing from a recipe belonging to his mother, a great Southern beauty and terrible cook, and hamburgers à la Betty Crocker's *New Boys and Girls Cookbook,* which he nicked when he moved out in 1978. Sort of boggles the mind, doesn't it, that that's the one he picked, scanning the built-in bookshelves as the Mayflower moving men were carrying the couch out the door? *The Art of French Cooking* his soon-to-be-ex-wife had worked her way through would have made a more dignified choice, but I think he had a hunch that he harbored no untapped reserves of culinary talent and, accordingly, aimed low. I can't shake the suspicion that most men in his situation, having furnished the bachelor pad with a set of cheap flatware and two pans, would either eat out every meal or eventually think, *Say, this cookbook of my daughter's consists primarily of little kids' party food. Think I'll drive over to the mall next Saturday and see if B. Dalton has something more suitable for a male divorcé in his late forties.* But not my father. Not Reed. He was content with his mother's chicken and the patties he mastered by following Betty's impossible-tobotch instructions, and for nearly two decades after I could count on him to drawl, as he ferried a platter of hamburgers the few feet from the kitchenette to the table, "Now, Miss Ayun, let me test your memory to see if you can tell me where I got this recipe."

"From my *Boys and Girls Cookbook,*" I would mutter.

"That's right! From your *Boys and Girls Cookbook!*" he'd echo happily, a conspiratorial gleam in his eye as he turned to include whoever else happened to be present, a friend of mine from high school or some wan bachelor he'd befriended at his new church. Even though he couldn't have cooked his way out of a bag of Jiffy Pop, he took to entertaining with a singular relish. He even managed to get himself invited to join a gourmet group, proudly noting that the other members had exempted him from cooking by appointing him permanent sommelier.

"You know," he'd tell our guest, "Back when I married Ayun's mother, I didn't have any reason to go into the kitchen. Betsy was a wonderful cook, I mean really!" The ice cubes in his gin and tonic rattled as he warmed to the subject. "Oh, I could grill steaks or open a can of Campbell's tomato soup," he'd continue airily. "But you know, I really didn't know how to cook anything. But now this cookbook of Ayun's, well, the recipes in there are nothing fancy, but by gum, they taste pretty good. So dig in." Somehow he always managed to make that jaunty "dig in" sound both confident and modest, the nonchalant shrug of the professional chef who throws together a light meal of langoustines braised with horse chestnuts when unexpected company drops in at midnight.

As my father intimated, and Darla's Enchanted Castle made distressingly clear, most of the recipes in Betty Crocker's *New Boys and Girls Cookbook* relied heavily on prepackaged mixes.

Ingredients-wise, the Castle was nothing more than a dessert version of the Kwik 'n' Tastee casseroles dominating the women's magazines, the ones my mother failed to condemn when going on record in the *Indianapolis Star* as thinking that men preferred steak. Instead of such savories as Campbell's cream of mushroom and Campbell's cream of celery, it called for packages of yellow cake mix and "fluffy white frosting." I hope I'm not coming across as some sort of anti–cake mix zealot. Despite a lifelong bias toward from-scratch baked goods, I had nothing against powdered mix, as long as I could consume it on my own terms—i.e., by the spoonful, unreconstituted.

In first grade, the student body of the parochial school I attended was seized with a mania for Jell-O powder after one of our numbers remarked upon its similarity to Pixy Stix. At the end of the day, we'd sit on the floor outside the chapel, promiscuously dipping moistened fingers into those little rectangular boxes while waiting for our carpools to arrive. Naturally, this crude behavior inspired the wrath of our Anglican teacher-ladies, but they didn't dare inflict any of the diabolical punishments for which they were known so close to the moment when parents' station wagons would start pulling up out front. Confiscation was the worst that could happen. Even that wasn't too terrible, because my grandmother's pantry never lacked for Jell-O. It was the primary ingredient in most of her salads. I always felt so accomplished, sitting there on the linoleum of Saint Richard's, misusing this familiar product under the disapproving gazes of Miss Baker and Miss Huff. Nothing beats the satisfaction of making your own food, particularly when you're a kid and the only crucible you've got access to is your mouth.

Over the years, I would sometimes reflect on how my father had stolen my childhood cookbook, and, despite that old saw about possession being nine-tenths of the law, I wanted it back. *Let him copy his precious burger recipe onto an index card,* I thought. The book should be returned to its original owner, who now had children of her own. I wanted to be ready to heed the call to dazzle a table full of little kids with a whimsical birthday cake. I suppose I could have anted up for a brand-new copy, but what did I want with an updated edition, with souped-up photographs and no inscription? No facsimile would do, and yet, given his mellow response to such potentially parent-ruffling situations as straying from the church and throwing a party where my high school friends drained his liquor cabinet before nipping off to *Rocky Horror,* it seemed kind of petty to ask him to make a special trip to the post office just to return what was rightfully mine. It took a while, but finally I was able to seize on an opportunity to frame my request in a way that didn't make me feel too churlish, phoning my father up in Indianapolis.

"Listen, Daddy, the kids and I are going to be in town to collect the stuff that Grampy stored for me back when Greg and I moved to New York. I thought maybe, if it's convenient, we could have dinner."

"Oh, by all means. Now, tell me, what should I have on hand for the children to eat? Will Miss Inky eat hamburgers?"

"She might, or I was thinking maybe we could order pizza or something—"

"Oh, why, we certainly could, if that's what you think she would like. And now, what about Master Milo? Will he also want a pizza?" He's got this way of pronouncing it so that it almost sounds like the Leaning Tower of . . . like it's this exotic dish with which he has only passing familiarity.

"Daddy, Milo's seven months old. He eats baby food."

"Oh, well now, I think I could probably get that at the Safeway if you'll tell me what sort of thing he likes. Now what was it that you liked to eat when you were a baby? You were such a plump little thing. I've told you what we used to call you, haven't I?"

"Plumpy Plumpkins."

"That's right, Plumpy Plumpkins! Now, I can't remember what exactly it was, but when you used to see those little jars of whatever they were, strained pears or whatever . . . does it still come in little jars like that, baby food?"

"Still does, yeah." Oh my god, this was going to take all night if he insisted on pausing at every daisy sprouting up along Memory Lane. While my father laughed, delighted that such a thing as baby food jars could still exist in the twenty-first century, I cut to the chase, no more capable of etiquette than a driver whose car has stalled on the railroad tracks. "Anyway, what I was wondering is, do you still have my cookbook? The *Boys and Girls* one that Gran and Grampy gave me for my birthday?"

"Oh, that cookbook that Bob and Elva gave you, why, yes. You know those hamburgers that I make?"

"I know. I know where you got the recipe, but listen. I was thinking that I'd like it back, unless you're still using it."

"Why, no, you can have it. I'll have to write the hamburger recipe down before you take it away, though. You'd think I'd have the damn thing memorized by now!"

Or that, just once in twenty years, he'd have been moved to vary his routine, maybe take a stab at transforming the burgers into happy faces, as Betty does on page 45, or even head off into such uncharted territory as Chili Concoction or Fruit Basket Upset. Perhaps if I'd let him hold on to the book for another twenty years, he would have. Who knows? He could've surprised me with an Enchanted Castle for my sixtieth birthday.

When I finally got my cookbook back from Daddy, I tore through it, looking for the bunnies. They were the first dish I ever prepared on my own, not counting three ashtray-sized cakes made from the three pouches of mix that came with my Easy-Bake Oven. (My mother never got around to buying any refills, a move I now heartily condone.) As a young chef, I was disappointed that so many of the recipes in the book made use of the burners, sharp knives, and raw meat that unfortunately required adult supervision. Bunny Salad, however, was truly easy enough for a child—or maybe even Reed Halliday—to prepare. It was also hands-down adorable. It really looked like its namesake, which wasn't always the case. Rocket Salad, for instance, resembled not so much something on the launching pad of Cape Canaveral as a giant, maraschino cherry–tipped boner, not that I thought so at the time, of course. Back then, I just felt gypped that I couldn't get my banana to stand up, no matter how many toothpicks Gran suggested jamming into its base.

The bunnies, however, were completely compliant, making them a good choice for a child's first solo outing as a chef. Having banished my parents and grandparents to the dining room, I tied on an apron to arrange canned pear halves around a plate lined with purely decorative lettuce leaves, positioning the fruit with the narrow ends pointing toward the center. Next, I trimmed each hunkered-down pear body with raisin eyes, almond ears, a Red Hot nose, and a big, gaggy cottage cheese tail. Nestled sweetly on their bellies, their noses nearly touching, my creation looked so much like baby bunnies that I wanted to nuzzle one of them against my cheek. Instead, I carried the plate into the dining room, where my elders waited to devour the entire litter.

"Now tell me, Bob," my father demanded, sighting his then-father-in-law along the prongs of his fork. "Did you have any idea you had such a talented granddaughter?"

"Takes after her mother! She's the dickens, all right," Grampy agreed with stageworthy vigor. "Yessir, looks like we've got another gourmet in the family!"

"I should say," my father chimed back.

What a performance. Mom and Gran-Gran would never have laid on the ham sauce that thick. They were probably wondering if I'd left them a big mess to clean up, or perhaps praying, as I now do, that Little Picky wasn't developing big ideas about horning in on the sanctuary of their kitchens before developing some equally big ideas about eating everything on her plate. I'm sure all four of the adults were deflated when so much lavish praise, coupled with the satisfaction of having "cooked" something, failed to convince me to sample so much as one bite of that cottage cheese. I must have had them wrapped around my little finger, though, because not a single one had the steeliness to deny the finicky chef's "dessert hole."

Permit me to explain. When I was little more than a toddler, my grandmother tried to trick me into eating by dividing my body into a collection of "holes," situated along various abdominal checkpoints, far from any actual orifice. "Hmm," she would begin, two fingers prodding the designated spots as if she were some medieval apothecary assessing the humors. "Pear hole's still got some room. Better put some lima beans in your lima bean hole while you're at it. Fill that up too."

"What about my 'zert hole?" I'd countered, according to family legend. I may have borne a passing resemblance to Margaret O'Brian, the grave-faced 1930s child actress celebrated for her ability to cry on command, but in that moment, I was Shirley Temple. This gut response charmed the grownups to such a degree that from that moment on, they could never bring themselves to deny me dessert, though I did have to endure a lot of embarrassing "hole" talk in front of boyfriends and other assorted dignitaries in later years. Gran just couldn't let it go. Nor would she see fit to mention that sprawling in front of the fireplace, eating an entire batch of cookies, is a hobby a growing girl would do well to outgrow sooner rather than later. Deeply suspicious of drugs, rock music, teenage boys, and tube tops, she did her best to detain me in childhood for as long as possible by seizing every opportunity to baby my sweet tooth. A noble, if mostly failed, attempt.

Thirty-four years after it was given to me, the pictures of the sweeties in Betty Crocker's *New Boys and Girls Cookbook* still exert tremendous Pavlovian appeal, despite what I now know about the Enchanted Castle and the advisability of eating anything that lists "frosting mix" as a primary ingredient. I'm like an elderly gay gentleman who, after years of global sexual intrigue, takes perverse pleasure in pawing through the laughably wholesome physique mags that dominated his boyish imagination. How does that old saying go: One man's Kookie Kat

Sundae is another's crew-cut shot-putter a-frolic in his skivvies? Even though I'm glad to be in receipt of it, the truth is I didn't really need the book. All I have to do is close my eyes to conjure up those Ice Cream Flower Pots, the Grape Float, and all four varieties of fudge. I'm old enough now that I don't want to taste them. I want to taste what I once imagined they tasted like.

And I still find myself directing uncharitable feelings toward Betty's twenty-five child Test Helpers. Introduced by name in the front of the book as simpering pencil renderings, their job was to weigh in throughout with opinions and anecdotes about various recipes. How I hated them, those goody-two-shoed stooges whom fortune had seen fit to make famous and important, instead of me! I yearned for a cookbook scout to visit my school, in order that I might join their ranks and surpass them all, but none ever did. All I could do was stew about how much peppier my commentary would have been.

Leftover meatloaf makes the most wonderful sandwiches! Becky brownnosed. The exclamation mark following her dumpy hint made me want to slap her pretty cheek. I knew for a fact that the only thing leftover meatloaf could possibly make was something Cesar, a pride-free neighborhood Saint Bernard, would gobble with gusto from a dented pie plate Gran put out in the yard. Wonderful sandwiches, indeed! I could tell that Becky was one of those girls who'd say anything to remain in the teacher's good graces. Only now does it occur that maybe Becky chose the lesser of two evils, her comment a diversionary tactic engineered to get her out of giving a rave to the page's nauseating star attraction, Meatloaf à la Mode.

Kneading dough is just like playing with clay, Michael reported.

Only you can bake dough into something that's good to eat. I hope I won't give offense if I report that Michael's penciled portrait had the eight-year-old me convinced that he was borderline developmentally disabled.

If I were a mama, Elizabeth confided, *I'd cook all day.* Good for you, honey. How's that working out?

And then there was Joan, who looked like she cut her own hair with a butter knife and said of the Pink Popcorn Balls, *The pink makes the popcorn look pretty.* What was she, a baby? Pink Popcorn Balls might have been low on my list of recipes to try, but even so, I itched to supplant Joan's worthless commentary with some *Zoom*-influenced observations of my own. *Wow! Exploding with Crunchy* AND *Chewy Flavor! Like a Styrofoam ball you can eat but even crazier because it's* PINK! *I give these an A plus* PLUS *and so will you!*

(Here I feel compelled to state that the photograph of Pink Popcorn Balls vertically piled atop two obscenely large Chocolate-Caramel Apples rivals the erect phallus that is Rocket Salad.)

The mind boggled as to why Joan had been selected to represent the Enchanted Castle when the best she could muster was, *My father took a picture of me with my cake.* As Capote said of Kerouac, that's not writing. That's typing. Maybe she was Betty Crocker's niece, in which case she probably had the Enchanted Castle every year. Somehow, this did nothing to diminish my envy, the gnawing conviction that Betty Crocker and her minions had called off the search prematurely in Ohio. Like the proverbial Who, I hung around on my dust speck, pining to be noticed and possibly redeemed, given skills that would enable me to eat nothing but 'zert for the rest of my life.

shitty kitty confection

Little MoMo hipped me to this trompe l'oeil treat, which, true to the genre, leans on instant pudding and cake mix, allowing the chef to concentrate on such lofty matters as verisimilitude and shopping for pet supplies.

Prepare 1 large package of instant vanilla pudding mix according to package directions. Most likely this will involve milk. (You'll want to have some on hand anyway, to wash down the horrifyingly realistic finished product.) Stick the pudding in the fridge in a container of your choosing.

Mix 1 box of German chocolate cake mix with whatever eggs or oils it may call for, and bake according to the instructions on the side of the box in whatever size pan grabs you.

Repeat the above process with 1 box of white cake mix.

Get ready to fuck your blender up with 1 package of vanilla sandwich cookies . . . you know, the kind you hated as a kid because they weren't dark, like Oreos. If you're the old-fashioned type, get out your rolling pin and clobber them to crumb city that way.

If you want to get really fancy, dude up 1 cup of cookie crumbs with a few drops of green food coloring. Stir them up good and set aside.

Once the cakes have cooled, crumble them into your largest mixing bowl with half of the undyed cookie crumbs and enough pudding to bind it all together, without turning things too boggy.

Line the brand-new litter box you bought at the pet-supply store with one of the brand-new disposable litter box liners picked up on the same trip. This is one step where it doesn't pay to skimp, no matter how fastidiously you wash dishes.

Strip the wrappers off a few small Tootsie Rolls and heat them in a microwave until they are as pliant as if you'd tucked them into your armpits for an hour (which you can totally do if, like me, you don't have room for a microwave in your kitchen). Now that they're warm, these little brown logs are yours for the shaping. Pay special attention to the ends, which should be tapered. Make as many of them as you like, but at least one per guest. Follow your muse. Just work in small batches for maximum plasticity. Bury most of the doctored Tootsies in the cake mixture.

Over this mess, sprinkle the remaining undyed cookie crumbs. Fancy types can follow this up with judiciously spaced, chlorophyll green "odor crystal" crumbs.

For good measure, plop a few more Tootsies defiantly atop the "litter"—you know, the way felines do.

Serve with a pooper-scooper that, if not brand new, is at least reserved for culinary purposes such as this.

Daddy says it's just like Pussy makes, but twice as delicious!

—Joan

courtesy bite

Before we could eat, we had to say grace. In French.

"Benny say, 'Señor Key New Saw Prepare a Syrup Paw . . . '"

I droned phonetically with the rest of the kids, blindly accepting the suggestion that God's first name could be Benny. Even in private school, the spirit of inquiry only extends so far. I had other things to worry about, like whether the person in charge of our table would try to strong-arm me into the Clean Plate Club, and if so, please God, don't let the entrée be Salisbury steak. I'm begging you, Benny, *s'il-vous plait.*

Rumor had it that from seventh grade on, Park Tudor students could not only choose what they wanted to eat from a variety of options, but also where to sit and with whom. Those of us in the Lower School were subject to family-style dining, a policy that got played up in the school's brochure as just one more example of the differences between our "tradition of excellence" and the implied mayhem of a public, or even parochial, education. My parents proved susceptible enough to this sort of propaganda to transfer me from Saint Richard's in second grade. I was but a babe of seven when my new school's regulations forced me to bid goodbye to the Hostess cupcakes, Twinkies, and tiny cans of Snak-Pack pudding I'd grown accustomed to carrying in my lunchbox, a funky-smelling metal Disney school bus with matching thermos.

Jettisoning chocolate Zingers seemed an unfairly hefty fee to escape the tiny but lethal foil balls flying like shrapnel through the low-ceilinged room in which I had lunched all throughout kindergarten and first grade. The boys used to spend the first half of lunch collecting Ding Dong wrappers, a practice that enabled them to spend the second half whipping the aforementioned balls at the cowering female foil donors, the assistant rector, each other . . . everyone except Mitzi and Butch, two untidy mongrels who belonged to no one but had somehow obtained permission to wander the facilities unobstructed, licking hands and god knows what else.

That kind of shit, the brochure intimated, didn't have a snowball's chance in hell of going down at Park Tudor, because our food was hot, wholesome, and communal. Flying foil balls, spoiled dogs, and sour-smelling lunchboxes were not permitted anywhere near the grand, free standing dining hall we referred to as Clowes Commons, in honor of a local philanthropist who had also footed the bill for the large hall where the symphony orchestra and touring companies of Broadway musicals played. Just in case these high standards weren't formidable enough to squash anarchy in the bud, our seats were assigned, plotted specifically to divide and conquer even the rowdiest of troublemakers.

Permanently based at every table was a teacher or a sixth-grade girl charged with meting out discipline, fomenting appropriate conversation, and dishing up the meal her fifth-grade "waiter" had carried out from the kitchen. With just one representative per grade at every table, duties were clear-cut: Fourth graders fetched milk and, later, dessert. Third graders took care of tray stands and silverware. Second graders used sour-smelling, pink-striped Handi Wipes to clean the tables at the end of the meal. First graders ferried trash and, not infrequently, the napkin-wrapped retainers of older tablemates to a trio of industrial garbage cans, whose moist, reeking contents it was my pleasure to sort through on the two occasions my orthodontic appliance went missing.

Two weeks into any given lunchtime assignment, before significant alliances could form, everyone except the teachers and sixth-grade girls was rotated to a new position. Fifth graders skipped five tables, fourth graders four, and so on. As a shy, picky eater with no sibling experience, I lived in terror of this mandatory mad tea party. What I wouldn't have given to eat at my desk, like the lucky kindergartners, whose teachers were as pretty and kindhearted as Snow White and Rose Red. Anything that could get me out of the line of fire of Mrs. Hogarth, the pastel-haired punisher I would get to know better in fourth grade, the most miserable year of my educational career.

Unfortunately, doing time at Mrs. Hogarth's table was an inescapable rite of passage in the Tradition of Excellence. Far from being alarmed on my behalf, my parents seemed amused by this Dickensian trial, as if it were just one more thing Park Tudor was doing to prepare me for college. I rotated to Hogarth right on schedule, a couple of weeks before school let out for the hotly anticipated winter holidays. Clearly, the high seasonal spirits already infecting surrounding tables were not to be ours, as our hostess welcomed her new "family" with a plethora of

Hogarthian ground rules, chief among them that children would not speak unless spoken to. Thus did she guarantee that her opinions would go unchallenged as she filled the dead air surrounding the divvying up of pressed turkey roll and canned lima beans with scathing indictments of chewing gum, bell-bottoms, Wacky Packs, and Helen Reddy.

Finally, the headmistress mounted the stage to lead us in grace, after which Mrs. Hogarth lapsed into silence, her lips held tightly closed over her teeth as they ground away at a foul mouthful of beans. Like a mongoose hypnotized by a cobra's terrible majesty, I couldn't help noting that her cardigan was the exact same shade as the limas. I might have stayed transfixed forever had not a lively chorus struck up at a nearby table, presided over by a popular and permissive sixth grader named Julie.

This is the salt.

The what?

The salt.

The what?

The salt.

Oh, the salt!

I loved this game or, more accurately, round, which when performed correctly had all the beauty of synchronized swimming. I knew it wouldn't be long before the pepper, the ketchup, a spoon, a fork, a napkin-wrapped retainer, and anything else that could enter the fray would be chasing the saltshaker around the circular table, as voices and heads turned in unison. Unfortunately, Julie had failed to factor in the batlike ears of Mrs. Hogarth.

"Miss Peterson, if you do not put an immediate stop to the nonsense you are permitting to take place at Table Four, I will come do it myself," she snapped, "in which case I will also relieve you of your duties for the remainder of the year, since you so obviously lack the maturity to set an example worthy of following." Even knowing that we'd get in trouble for it, it was impossible to refrain from rubbernecking. I prayed that someone at the guilty table was hyperactive, deaf, or suicidal enough to keep the game going, but to my great disappointment, the whole lot of them bowed their heads as if saying a second grace. The whole spectacle was so chilling, I forced down a couple of lima beans while Julie, the sixth grader, flushed a bright, Christmasy red, trying not to cry.

Those sixth-grade girls exuded a glamour with which no teacher—except possibly Mrs. Knall, a tall drink of water in platform shoes, wire-rimmed glasses, and hoop earrings the size of Gainesburgers—could compete. How competent, carefree, and informed they seemed, making deft sport of everything from Bobby Riggs and the bald woman on the cover of the Ohio Players' album to the noxious reconstituted mashed potato fumes unfurling from the kitchen. Half the time, I didn't have an inkling what they were talking about, but I could barely wait until I, too, would be mistress of my own table, dropping impressively casual references to perverts and potheads, granting exemption from courtesy bites to any pitiful soul claiming an allergy to succotash. As far as I was concerned, the only thing wrong with sixth-grade girls was their inability to control fifth-grade boys.

For two interminably long weeks, the mad tea party dictated that I share a table with the most popular boy in fifth grade, a cold-eyed, Roman-nosed murderer whose ski jacket's zipper pull bristled with lift tickets. His proximity wouldn't have been so alarming with Mrs. Hogarth at the helm, but this was February, and the sixth grader running this show was best friends with the murderer's sister. To my great astonishment, she behaved as if she found his insults and vulgarity endearing.

"Oh, sick, Jenny, did you see that?" he yelled in the middle of the meal one day.

"No, what?" our hostess asked, looking up eagerly.

"That kid just picked an enormous green booger out of his nose and ate it!" he announced, pointing at the third grader seated directly across from me.

"Did not!" the accused protested loudly, dropping his fork.

"Yes you did, I saw you."

"I didn't! I swear!"

"Did too. Why make it worse by lying about it?"

"I'm not lying," the third grader insisted, his face contorting in frustration and grief.

"Ooh, now the little baby's going to cry about it?"

"I'm not crying!"

"Does the little baby want his dy-dee changed?"

"Andy-Panda, you're so mean," our sixth grader giggled in—could it be?—admiration. "Ignore him, Lyman. He can't help being a retard. Can you, Andy-Panda?" She leaned over to ruffle the murderer's fashionably long hair.

"At least I'm not the one gobbling up boogers," he retorted, grinning as he mopped some ketchup off his plate with a tater tot, his appetite apparently unaffected by the recent unpleasantness. I, on the other hand, felt as if I might throw up at any moment, though to have done so would have earned me a lasting association nearly as hideous as that of poor Lyman, the Green Booger Boy.

Years later, when a friend mentioned that Andy-Panda had cut off two of his fingers in a lawn-mowing accident, I immediately thought in terms of karmic retribution. Not so much on behalf of Lyman, who no doubt would have received the grisly news with a gladness even grimmer than mine, but because of banana pudding, which Andy-Panda forever ruined by likening it to "girl crap." Apparently, "monkey pus" wasn't malevolent enough for the likes of him; no, he had to undermine a prepubescent girl's confidence in the sanctity of her own body. Thanks, Andy-Panda!

Nine years old, completely ignorant of menstruation and where babies came from, I now began to live in terror that one day I'd start dispensing a jiggly, pale-yellow substance from one hole or another. And that, somehow, the second that it happened, the fiend would find out and immediately share the news with whatever table was now lucky enough to be enjoying his company. What a horrible sadist that kid was. At least when the mountainous Mrs. Bailey ate the compost she scraped from her traumatized charges' plates prior to sending their dirty trays back to the kitchen, she was driven by gluttony, not some deep-seated impulse to torture.

Finally, after four years in the trenches, I crept to the head of the class and was given my own table, Number Two, conveniently located by the two-story windows and Mrs. Hogarth. What a shocker to claw my way up through the ranks, only to discover that portioning out bad food to younger kids whose status had no bearing on mine wasn't really the great honor I'd always assumed it to be. Knowing that girls just one year my senior, peers whom I remembered slaughtering me in bombardment just a few months prior, were now middle schoolers who got to eat lunch with friends at tables of their choosing siphoned off a lot of the glamour. I felt less the de facto mother of the broods assigned to me every two weeks than the oldest peanut in the peanut gallery. With my back to the windows, I gazed across platters, tureens, and tray stands, sending surreptitious nonverbal signals to my friends Molly, Marybeth, and Casey.

"Can you believe the suckiness of it all?" we told each other with our eyes. "I hate these barfy corn dogs and stupid French grace. The second grader at my table is so disgusting. His nose won't stop running. I bet you wish you were sitting with Todd E! I wish I were sitting with you!" These silent exchanges seemed way more vital than any real-life banter taking place at my table.

I think I did a fairly good job of protecting the weak that year, if only because of the crippling reticence that struck me whenever I found myself in spitting distance of lippy, lift ticket–sporting males. Their watches, I noticed, tended to wind down rather quickly when they weren't egged on. Knowing that Mrs. Hogarth had me under surveillance, I doled out the expected number of courtesy bites, as impervious as an emergency room nurse to the garden-variety pain this practice caused. If a younger kid appeared on the verge of a conniption fit, I might show myself capable of mercy, whispering that it was okay to hide the four peas I'd dealt her beneath her unfinished pork cutlet, but only if she could do so without attracting teacherly attention. As a sixth-grade girl, I found lunch much the same as I found driving to Florida with Gran, Grampy, and my mother: endless, boring scenery broken up by the occasional low-level accident.

Once the applause at a dropped tray had died down, it was back to the tedium of the road, the pleasures of my destination too many miles away to get worked up about. (At that point, I still equated seventh grade with Disney World.) The most memorable event of my hostessly tenure was the headmistress shouting at me to tell my fifth-grade waiter, an expressive, good-humored, effeminate blond, to "stop shaking his long hair all over the food." Fashionably uncropped tresses were tolerated on macho specimens like Andy-Panda, but the whimsy of the nellier fellows who dared to sport this look invariably brought out the worst in faculty battle-axes. Despite what the brochure claimed to nurture, ours was never a particularly arts-friendly environment. The football team sucked too. Even when pitted against the Indiana School for the Deaf.

Almost as soon as I attained seventh grade's longed-for lunch-period freedoms, I skidded to the unpleasant realization that all students were defined and categorized by their lunch choices according to a code I was ill-equipped to crack. Only through trial and error did I come to understand, if not master, the unspoken rules. Lunchboxes were for babies. Sack lunches from home were acceptable, provided they contained nothing weird and were supplemented by potato chips or sandwich cookies from the racks near the cashiers. Prepaid lunch tickets were queer if you were a girl, but okay if you were a boy. Begging lunch tickets off boys by whining, squealing, and hitting was considered a celebrated trait in any girl popular enough to act this way on a regular basis. Girls who bought their lunches at school should confine themselves to oyster crackers, fruit, and the aforementioned chips and cookies, but boys were free to consume a square meal, complete with side dishes and dessert. The black kids ate together by the windows. The teachers would intervene only if violence threatened or some loudmouth persisted in shouting the word "dick." Otherwise, they remained sequestered around a gloomy table in the back, drinking coffee, eating the daily specials and pointedly ignoring the nut jobs who made their working hours a living hell. The only ritual that carried over from Lower School was the applause that greeted a dropped tray.

"Look, Casey thinks she's so big because she's sitting at Tina Tyler's table," my friend Molly whispered, working to denude her chicken noodle soup of sliced celery.

"I know, it's so sad," I muttered, taking a bite of the cream cheese and olive sandwich I had brought from home out of loyalty to my mother. She'd been so excited to send me off that first day of seventh grade with a replica of the lunch that had been her favorite, back when girls wore saddle shoes and didn't sit with boys. "It's like she's too dumb to realize they don't even like her."

"In gym, she was all bragging about how she got invited to Steve Parker's bar mitzvah."

"I'm so sure." I took a frowning sip from my half-pint carton of orange drink. For years Casey Malone had counted as one of my best friends, but lately she'd started behaving like she wanted nothing further to do with me. "She probably thinks Steve's going to ask her to 'go' with him."

"Are you going to Melissa's on Saturday?" one of the other girls at our table asked.

"I guess so," Molly murmured, as diplomatically as possible, given the circumstances. I busied myself with stripping the cellophane from a packet of peanut butter crackers.

"Ayun, are you?"

The social order was shifting in ways I couldn't fathom. I knew Melissa much better than I knew my interlocutor, an agreeable but dim mouth-breather notable primarily for having a Winnebago in the family. Why would she have some line on spending the night at Melissa's? Why would Molly know what she was talking about?

"Uh, I don't know," I answered, casting about the vast Commons for any distraction that might serve to reroute this unnerving conversation. "Oh my god, you guys, look! Madame Tarkovsky's flirting with that greasy-haired cashier guy!" My companions shifted their attention to the checkout line, where our French teacher fumbled in her purse as the cashier waited impassively for payment.

"She's got the hots for his long fingernails," Molly said loyally, no doubt as relieved as I for a change of subject. "They turn her on."

"Hey, do you want to go back? I forgot something in my locker that I need for gym."

"Are you kidding? I just finished getting rid of this celery."

*

I hadn't known how good we'd had it back in Lower School, when the assigned seating arrangement precluded all possibility of clustering with our peers. Once, when Molly was out with the flu, I panicked and made a beeline for the first ally I could identify, lest one of the popular kids see me hesitating in the middle of the floor. "Hi, Casey," I said, drawing up alongside a table not far from the teachers', where my old friend had alighted with some of her new cronies.

"Oh. Hi." Casey took a slurp of her Tab. It was a popular-girl thing to buy soda from the vending machine in the gym and keep it in your purse until lunch.

"That seat's saved," hissed Lissa Lucas as I set my tray down in an unoccupied spot. Lissa Lucas was Tina Tyler's best friend. For some reason, all the fast girls who'd transferred from the public elementary schools for seventh grade had feathered hair and alliterated names, just like Farrah Fawcett, whose red-nippled likeness was everywhere at the time. "You can't sit there."

"Oh. Okay." I picked up my tray and attempted to wriggle through the narrow channel in between Casey's chair and the chair back of the kid seated behind her.

"No, you can't sit there, either." Lissa stabbed a green banana in my direction as if activating an invisible force field.

"Who's sitting there?" I asked, even though I sort of knew. My fingers tightened on my tray. Casey folded her arms and glared. A couple of the others flicked their bangs as knowing glances were exchanged.

"No one!" Lissa said. "We just don't want you here. This is a private table. Understand? Or are you dense?" This from someone who used her fingers to count in math class, who didn't even know colors in French!

If only I had had the balls to smash my tray into her face, I'd have delivered a blow so stinging she'd be lucky to retain the use of her legs. The teachers would have to come splashing through a spreading puddle of my spilled orange drink. It'd take at least three of them to pull me off her scratched and broken body. "Who's so tuff now?" I'd scream, brandishing the moussed tufts I'd separated from her scalp. "Say it! Why don't you say it, huh?"

"Mademoiselle Halliday, *ma petit chou-fleur, calmez-vous!*" Madame Tarkovsky would beg, secretly pleased to see a long-standing upholder of Park Tudor traditions teaching this insolent newcomer a thing or two.

How awesome would that have been?

Instead, I staggered two feet away, skidded on an AWOL crinkle-cut fry, then turned back toward Casey to bleat, "I thought you were my friend!"

"Well, that was then," she shrugged, reaching across to help herself to one of Lissa's Fritos.

"Oh my god, you guys, did you see?" I heard one of them say as I beat a swift retreat, praying I'd reach the stairs before I could disgrace myself further. "She was crying."

Jeez, maybe if they'd kept assigned seating in the upper grades, I'd have been drawn to a respectable career in finance or law instead of theater, with its tantalizing whiff of one day making the Lissa Lucases of the world curdle with feelings of worthlessness and inadequacy. *Just think how bad they'll*

feel, I thought, *when they flip on their televisions to see me accepting my Academy Award in a midnight blue sequined dress with spaghetti straps and a handkerchief hemline.* Theater granted a bit of perspective on my unexpected fall from grace: Let the cheerleaders flock together in their ridiculous little skirts, bumming lunch tickets from loutish tight ends like the as-yet-unmutilated Andy-Panda! They might consider themselves hot snot on a silver platter, but one day they'd regret not letting me sit with them. "If only we'd have known she was going to be so famous!" they'd cry in their ridiculous little baby-doll voices. So what if Casey Malone didn't say hello when she cruised past me towing twenty dollars worth of oversized helium balloons toward some other member of Sub-Deb, a secret sorority from which I—also secretly—was stricken to be excluded. To hell with them. I was headed for bigger and better things, like the chorus of *The Music Man* and the role of the main character's mother in *Our Town*.

My involvement in the drama club also ensured I always had someone to sit with when Molly got assigned to a different lunch period because she signed up for chemistry and calculus instead of music and art.

My new compatriots weren't the people I'd anticipated sitting with, back when I was in Lower School, but their dispositions were not wholly dissimilar from mine, and given that most of them had attended Park Tudor since they were in Healthtex, they knew how to play "This Is the Salt."

"Oh my god, they are so weeyurd," Lissa Lucas was overheard gasping to Tina Tyler. "Do you see what they're doing with that saltshaker?" Casey Malone sat as close to Tina as she could get, curling her lip as if she, too, had no idea what kind of queerball, baby, theater-type stuff was going on at Table Number Twelve, where not so long ago Mrs. Bailey, the Human Disposal, had presided . . . in fact, still presided every day at 11:15, the Lower Schoolers' traditional lunch period.

My fingers closed around the first thing I could think to grab. "This is the Tab," I announced firmly.

"The what?" my former fifth-grade waiter simpered, shaking his long hair.

"The Tab." Fuck those stupid middle school bitches calling us "weeyurd."

"The what?" He raised his eyebrows politely as his hand joined mine on the fuchsia can I had purchased after gym.

"The Tab," I repeated, as emphatically as the established rhythm would allow.

"Oh," he confirmed, smiling in recognition. "The Tab."

miss leslie ayun miller's banana pudding

I've adapted this recipe from one that's been in my editor's family ever since one of her ancestors providently copied it off the side of a can. What a pity I'll never taste it.

Plug in the mixer and spend a minute beating a 14-oz can of sweetened condensed milk and 1½ cups of ice-cold water.

Add a small box of instant vanilla pudding and whale on it for another 2 minutes.

Unplug the mixer before licking the beaters.

Before you leave for school, refrigerate, covered.

When you come home, plug the mixer back in and whip 2½ or, for those in need of further fattening up, 3 cups of heavy cream until you get those lovely soft peaks that make you want to go skiing, even if you don't ski. Gently fold into the chilled pudding.

Slice four bananas.

Here's a little cheer, if you want one:

Lean to the left, lean to the right
Peel your banana and mmm! Take a bite!

Select a bowl big enough to serve 1 representative from every grade, plus a teacher.

Distribute ⅓ of a box of Nilla Wafers over the bottom of the bowl.

Cover the wafers with ⅓ of the sliced bananas.

Cover with ⅓ of the pudding, and continue distributing layers until no more layers remain.

Stretch some cling wrap over the top of the bowl, stick it in the fridge, and go play for at least three hours, but no more than eight.

If anyone mentions girl crap, threaten them with a lawn mower.

gnaw bone

After the pottery studio, the lake, the bunny hutch, and the cable swing, my favorite place at camp was the mess hall. The din in that room was constant, the activity level high. Screen doors slammed, benches scraped across the wooden floor, and kids bounded back and forth from the milk machine. Every few minutes, a teenage counselor would dump another dish towel of freshly washed cutlery into the metal bin at the head of the cafeteria line. If the Wonder Bread delivery truck crunched up the gravel driveway, everyone raced to the windows to see. At Gnaw Bone, you didn't have to ask for permission to be excused. We were free to put our elbows on the table, talk with our mouths full, break into song. The freewheeling energy of the place reminded me of the mess tent on *M*A*S*H*, an impression that only deepened as campers who'd arrived in Danskin short sets took to dressing in the rolled-up army fatigues that Fred, the camp director, warehoused in the rafters of the recreation building.

Fred couldn't get enough of that Army surplus. The broad flat handles of our knives were stamped US ARMY in a utilitarian font reminiscent of branding, an extremely popular camp activity. (Lacking a herd, we tagged scrap wood.) For some reason, these Army surplus knives had been designed with a hole at the end of their shafts, a feature that enabled us to twirl our utensils around our index fingers like six-shooters. Unhitched from the yoke of what our parents referred to as "acceptable behavior," we gargled our milk, then guffawed and burped as loudly as we could.

Every summer, I'd go from shy only child to badass urchin, part of a pack. Goodbye, obedient wearer of Danskin stretch-knit shells. Hello, unbrushed, Army-fatigued rugrat! My coach turned back into a pumpkin at the end of the annual two-week session, but the following July, I'd transform right back, thanks to a magical combination of fresh air, fellowship, the illusion of autonomy, and the fact that none of the counselors gave a shit if we cleaned our plates. Our teenage keepers wouldn't have cared if we ate nothing but Pop-Tarts.

Would that I could have obliged, but unfortunately, even at camp Pop-Tarts had been classified as an exclusively AM food. I'd developed an addict's preoccupation with the brand-name toaster pastry after supping freely on them at a well-stocked friend's house. My mother, whom I'd expected to disapprove, revealed herself to be a bit codependent by agreeing to let Pop-Tarts replace cinnamon toast in my morning routine. Perhaps she fell for that eight essential vitamins and minerals malarkey. Or maybe she didn't want to screw with a good thing, knowing that breakfast was the one meal of the day I could be counted on to consume in its entirety and without complaint, provided there were no nasty surprises like bacon, eggs, or anything requiring maple syrup. It was also essential that the table be set consistently: Count Chocula at six o'clock; cinnamon toast/Pop-Tart at eight; Nestlé's Quik (hot or cold, depending on the season) at eleven; grape juice at one; and a Pals vitamin, preferably the one shaped like the turtle, at two. I also had allegiances to various bowls, mugs, and place mats. Too bad I wasn't born twenty years later; I could have gotten myself labeled obsessive-compulsive.

At camp I woke with the whippoorwills, dressed quietly, and slunk down to the mess hall to play a couple rounds of solo tetherball while waiting for the cooks to come fire up my first 'Tart of the day. Once things got underway, the supply seemed endless, piling up on a sled-sized aluminum tray, from which we were expected to help ourselves. Never quite able to shake my anxiety that the bounty might one day prove finite, I snatched them up three at a time, inhaling them in my urgency to rejoin the line before they ran out, which, to my great relief, they never did.

With nature's most perfect breakfast food in such abundance, it amazed me that many of my fellow campers voluntarily squandered valuable plate and stomach space on scrambled eggs or, even more vomitrociously, sausage patties. What in the name of Indiana limestone was motivating these turkeys? Was it something to do with kickball, or hiking, or some other nonaquatic exertion spelling humiliation and discomfort for an uncoordinated, bunny-petting lanyard-weaver like myself? Did they not realize that our days were numbered, that soon we would be cast out of this culinary Eden, subject again to our parents' and teachers' dietary laws? I spent most of my time away from Gnaw Bone anticipating the freedoms of my annual two-week session, sniffing deeply of the Cutter bug repellent I sprayed on my forearms in an attempt to give substance to memories that in the dead of midwinter felt very far removed.

*

Decades in the business had shaped Fred's philosophy of camping, which was remarkably successful, despite this being the swinging seventies and he a gray-haired representative of the Greatest Generation. His rustic acreage featured an archery field, a horse corral, rope swings aplenty, a campfire pit surrounded by split log seating, all the traditional trappings that made parents express envy and nostalgia, but there were ways in which the Gnaw Bone experience was unique. School friends returning from Pokagon or Camp Waycross never spoke of clearing brush, exploring nearby abandoned buildings, or repairing tractors, all interests of Fred's that we were encouraged to share. We tagged along when he attended farm auctions, examining broken rakes and boxes of buttons while he bid on items I hadn't realized the average citizen could buy, most notably a soft-serve ice cream machine.

Shortly after this purchase, he pimped us out to rural neighbors whose end-of-season strawberry crops, too straggly to warrant professional picking, nonetheless yielded a staggering amount of fruit, which the farmer split with the child labor. That evening, dessert was dispensed from the mess hall's mud porch, where the soft-serve machine had been given a place of honor. Fred marched back and forth, gesturing to the strawberry sundaes the counselors were throwing together at a furious pace. "Why, the fellow down at the Dairy Queen would charge you more than a dollar for one of these," he boasted. "I'd say it tastes better free!"

Once, he took an ax to a dead raccoon he found on the side of the road, while the daughters of Central Indiana's professional class raced to call dibs on the feet Fred had declared "lucky." The man could brook no waste. I'll bet the only thing that kept that footless coon out of the Sloppy Joe pot was its size. From a distance, it was big enough to be mistaken for one of the breedless, much-stroked camp dogs, but even taking Hamburger Helper into account, it was no match for the appetites of seventy-five growing girls and their teenage counselors.

"Don't start out with a big helping," Fred boomed whenever we filed past the counter separating the kitchen from the dining area. "What if you don't like it? Start with a small taste, then come back for seconds and thirds." This approach was honey to my ears, especially since the initial sampling Fred promoted was in no way obligatory. If we wanted, we could give the whole damn line a miss and head straight for the Wonder Bread. That's what I did, feeling in no way deprived as I passed on spaghetti and meatballs or hamburgers or whatever children my age allegedly liked. Bread was the staff of life, was it not? I liked to dude mine up with white sugar, poured fast and loose from a screw-top glass receptacle. If only Mom and Gran could have seen fit to let me serve myself like this.

"You're so gross!" the egg-eaters seated near me on the screened-in side porch screamed as I gritted down on yet another glittering slice, producing a sound uncannily close to that of boots on crusted snow. "At least put some butter on it!" Butter? Disgusting. In my world, "butter" meant margarine, a substance whose only redeeming feature lay in the cleverness of television commercials for Imperial and Parkay.

"That your dinner or your dessert?" Fred asked, stepping onto the porch.

"It's my hors d'oeuvre," I whispered, stricken. Our counselors were teenagers, but Fred, when you came down to it, was a bona fide adult and, for these two weeks, my parents' proxy on all matters related to my health. His tendency to treat us more like enlisted men than children was flattering, but it now occurred to me that this might have its dark side. I expected that I'd be banned from sugar bread from here on out, but what if he forced me to start participating in softball? How I regretted the brazenness with which I had displayed my concoction. "Taste good to you?" Fred pressed, toying with me, enjoying his power. I nodded miserably, plucking at the hem of the field jacket I'd taken to wearing twenty-four hours a day. "Well, that's what counts!" he thundered, banging out the screen door to survey the kickball field.

God, I loved camp.

Feasting on sugar was hardly limited to mealtime. Twice a day, a bell summoned us to a wonderful thing called "commissary." At the start of the session, parents had the option of depositing funds in a commissary account that would allow their camper to "purchase" candy after swim and before campfire. Perhaps because I had no siblings, I always felt hesitant to ask my parents for gum, quarters for the pinball machine, and all the minor expenses my friends treated as their due. I could never have brought myself to lobby for something so extraordinary as the candy of my choice, dispensed twice daily for fourteen days, but fortunately, my father saw all the other fathers coughing up an extra ten bucks for their children's commissaries and did likewise without comment. I was in!

I spent a good portion of every swim session drifting around the lake on an Army surplus inner tube, deliberating on what to choose from the bulk candy cartons the commissary counselors would set out upon our return. Fads sprang up around the preferences of popular campers, but for the most part, I preferred to explore the unwholesome fringes. As much as I loved chocolate, I couldn't help gravitating toward whatever would last the longest. My miserly side was attracted to things that came in multiple units: Sprees, Sweet Tarts, Hot Tamales, and Bottle Caps, which looked like their namesake and tasted nothing like the root beer, orange soda, and cola they were supposed to, though they did seem vaguely carbonated, provided one ate enough of them. My temperament steered me toward the Stix family. Stix came in many flavors, Green Apple and Fire being my favorites, and were basically just Jolly Ranchers elongated into six-inch lengths. They shattered easily, were difficult to separate from their cellophane wrappers, and gave a satisfyingly loud report when bitten, though clearly, they'd been designed for sucking. In other words, they were perfect.

Long after my bunkmates had wolfed down their frozen Snickers, my stick, honed to lethal pointiness, continued to give pleasure. When the bell rang for dinner, I'd refold the torn cellophane over the inch or so remaining and tuck it away under the eaves, between my flashlight and the bottle of apricot-scented Earthborn for which I had snubbed Prell, our de facto family shampoo. While I was out, my candy stash would invariably attract swarms of tiny brown ants, whom I'd later discover partying like Bacchants beneath the untidy wrapper.

Nature's invasion would have amounted to tragedy had it happened at home where there was no commissary, but here I could head for the trash pail with an unemotional, if revolted, shrug. At camp, there was always more where that came from, for me as well as the ants, by no means the only species to benefit from my culinary largesse. Stabled on the way to the lake were a half dozen horses whom Fred had rescued from the glue factory to give trail rides and near-orgasmic grooming pleasure to a phalanx of horse-obsessed little girls who hung around the tack room, claiming to love the smell. An inexperienced hand like myself, who couldn't tell a pommel from a withers, stood little chance of getting close to these beasts during scheduled activity time, not when each animal was attended by two or three jealous equi-maids competing for favored wife status by kissing the fuzzy muzzles in a manner I found unhygienic and disturbing. I had to wait until watermelon days, when I raced through my sugar bread in order to beat the crowd to the rind bucket. Carrying it to the barn was privilege enough to warrant a skipped dessert.

"Uh . . . Prince?" I'd call tentatively, feeling it presumptuous of me to address any of them by name. "Gypsy?" In the horses' big, bulging eyes, I was a nobody, some peon from the pottery area. "I've brought you some delicious watermelon." The inedible-to-humans leftovers in my pail probably tasted closer to unripe honeydew, but who were these nags to discriminate? Unless one counted the handfuls of grass and leaves their devotees pushed through the bars of the corral fence, all they ever got was hay. A rusty bucket of watermelon rinds was a delicacy. As cascades of horse-scented slobber coursed down my forearms from their massive, grinding jaws, I did my best to convey my intentions telepathically. I wouldn't try to saddle them or brush them or keep other admirers from riding them. All I wanted was to feed them, and also for them not to accidentally bite my fingers off when they went for the crescent-shaped offerings. "Good girl, Missy," I whispered. "Nice horsey."

The reason the horses ate so much was that they spent their entire lives outdoors. Fred assigned mystical, appetite-enhancing properties to Gnaw Bone's smog-free Brown County air. "Spend all year cooped up with the television and the junk food, no wonder you're puny!" he'd tell whimpering, homesick recruits. "You don't know it, of course, but the only thing wrong with you is that you don't spend enough time in the Great Outdoors!" Fred loved the Great Outdoors even more than Army surplus. One night at campfire, he told us not to bother heading for the mess hall the next morning. "I ran into my old friend Mother Nature, and she said to bring everybody by for breakfast tomorrow," he said. "Look at little O'Malley over there. She doesn't know what I'm talking about. No, don't ask your neighbor. You'll find out soon enough if you don't stay up all night, telling ghost stories and bothering the guy who's trying to sleep."

The next morning, the counselors flushed us from our sleeping bags early so we could hump frying pans, hundreds of eggs, and a dozen family packs of bacon halfway to the lake for a breakfast cookout. Each cabin was responsible for its own share of the grub, which we were to prepare on a fire started not with matches, but with flint and steel.

"Tastes better when you cook it yourself!" Fred hollered every few minutes. Unfortunately, our counselor was having trouble coaxing so much as a spark from the file she clanged furiously with our rock. Naturally, every kid in Cedar Lodge had her own ideas about how to kindle a roaring blaze from a heap of damp pine needles fetched when the sun was low and hopes were high. The aroma of wood smoke and then frying meat permeated the air as we rocked anxiously on our heels, pelting our harried counselor with unwanted suggestions.

"Maybe if you rub the stone back and forth really quick instead of hitting it."

"Maybe if you do it backwards."

"I could go stick a stick in Ellen's fire and then bring it back!"

"Would you guys shut up for a second? God!" Our counselor yelled, yanking up the hood of her red IU sweatshirt. By now, most of the other cabins were enjoying paper plates of burnt toast and brownish eggs scrambled in bacon drippings.

"Tastes better when you cook it outdoors!" Fred shouted, kicking open a rotten log for an impromptu nature lesson on the squirming, scuttling, and now homeless creatures within. The temperature dropped noticeably and it started to sprinkle. And, again, call it kismet, call it camp magic, but I found myself a changed girl, salivating for that fire to get going so I could get me a big quivery lump of eggs shot through with bits of shell and stray blades of grass. Suddenly bacon sounded so good, I could have eaten it raw (and almost did, since the tiny fire Michelle finally got going with Fred's assistance died shortly after it ignited). I didn't want sugar on my white bread. I wanted it branded with the black stripes of a dented, rusty grill! Damn straight things tasted better outdoors, not to mention away from home, without silverware and in the rain, the unmistakable odor of horses mingling with the smoky aroma of a 100 percent Pop-Tart-free breakfast.

quiche

I've yet to really master the art of scrambling eggs, but I make a pretty mean quiche, which is actually much easier to hump into the wilderness, provided you bake it at home. It may taste *better outdoors, but have you ever tried to roll out piecrust on a rotten log?*

Bake a piecrust. I used to believe in those premade ones from the freezer case, but now I believe in bragging about how easy they are to make from scratch (recipe follows).

Preheat the oven to 350°.

Beat 3 eggs in a largish bowl that's not hell to pour things out of.

Add 1 cup of milk, 1 cup of cream, ¾ teaspoon of salt, and a couple grinds of pepper.

Chop some vegetables smaller than you usually would, enough to yield 1¼ cups. Big, stalky customers like broccoli or asparagus will require a blanching. Onions and shallots would benefit from a quick sauté in butter. Bacon's not a vegetable, but there's no denying it spent a couple of years as my number-one quiche ingredient.

Heap 1¼ cups of grated cheese in the middle of the piecrust. Pretend you're making one of those science experiments where baking soda comes bubbling out the top of a volcano.

Pour your egg mixture over the cheese.

Bake for 40 minutes or until a knife inserted in the center comes out clean. (If, after 40 minutes, the center remains liquid, don't freak. Sing a couple choruses of "The Titanic" and check back in a few minutes. Eventually, that sucker's got to firm up.)

Let it rest on the counter (or rotten log, if you insist) for 10 minutes. For those who care about appearances, this will make it much easier to serve. If you don't give a raccoon's ass for presentation, dig in!

HOMEMADE piecrust

In a large bowl, mix 1½ cups of flour (up to half of this can be whole wheat), ½ teaspoon of salt, and 1 teaspoon of sugar.

Cut in ¾ cup of shortening (it's awful for you and goes rancid fast!) and 4½ tablespoons of butter, broken into pieces. You can use a pastry cutter, a mixer, a food processor, or even two forks, like me.

Sprinkle 7 tablespoons of ice water over the coarse meal you've created and mush it together with your hands. Then roll it out, drape it over the pie plate, cover it with a sheet of tinfoil, weigh that down with a couple cups of dried beans, and bake in a 350° oven—which is the same temperature you'll need for the quiche, so don't turn the oven off.

child's plate

Long before I loved to eat, I loved to eat out. Restaurants hopped with life outside the family cocoon. The fancy ones made it easy to pretend that I was Sara from *A Little Princess*, before her father died in one of his diamond mines, forcing her to play servant to the cruel classmates who had begrudged her her wealth, beauty, and sterling disposition. The more informal spots had windows where kids could watch the chefs tossing their pizzas up in the air. The best kind piped in the sort of music my idol, Suzy Allerdice, the teenager next door, lived for. Even Hollyhock Hill, an Indianapolis institution I wouldn't hesitate to recommend to David Lynch's location scouts, had nifty features like mouthwash-colored mint sundae sauce and a cigar-store Indian in the spotlit bushes. Going out shook things up. My mother and grandmother remained seated as food was cooked, served, and cleared. My father and grandfather fumbled with their wallets, clumsily calculating tips. If a bowl of pastel pillow mints was stationed near the exit, everyone would take the spoonful to which they were entitled, then hand them off to me. But more than anything, going out was *way* synonymous with the possibility of grape Fanta.

Soda was a rare treat in my world. The only time my parents touched the stuff was Saturday lunch, when Coca-Cola was served on trays in the yard my father had spent all morning mowing. They seemed to relish it as much as I did, but not so much that it supplanted gin and tonics as their drink of choice, and certainly not enough for them to relax the rules. The rest of the week, Coke-drinking was strictly off-limits, a regulation I didn't dare breach, sensing that my mother might have a good handle on exactly how many cans remained after Saturday's dose had been decanted.

One of Gran's prized possessions was a framed sampler stating IF MOTHER SAYS NO, ASK GRANDMOTHER, but unfortunately, Gran didn't stock Coke. Like bikinis and *Chico and the Man*, it was just one of those things that raised her hackles. In high school, I once goaded her into taking a drink from a can I'd purchased after class. One sip and she dumped the remaining contents of her glass onto the grass, declaring, "That tastes like donkey dust!" My other grandmother, Missy, drank Tab, and when I visited her at her downtown apartment, I did too, figuring that it was at least the same color as Coke. I could also claim a passing familiarity with orange pop, thanks to vending machines in beauty parlors, auto-repair shops, and other places where a soda-less child soon descends into whining, but even that neon nectar paled in comparison to grape Fanta.

As far as I knew, the only place to get it was Rene's French Restaurant in Broad Ripple, a pleasant neighborhood that was as close as Indianapolis came to a bohemian sector. Sitting on one of Rene's mismatched wooden chairs, alternating nibbles of ridged potato chips with swigs from a can of grape Fanta, I felt in control of my own story. In French class, Madame had told us that boys and girls from France were allowed to drink watered-down wine with their dinner. My Fanta struck me as an equally sophisticated beverage, the kind of thing not every child was capable of handling. It seemed quite likely my fellow diners would mistake me for someone my mother was meeting for lunch, rather than her eight-year-old daughter. *If they were related*, the other customers would think, *that woman would have told the waitress to bring the little girl a glass of milk.* Milk, bah.

At Rene's, I forgot that I was the kid teachers referred to as "the shy one," ordering cans of Fanta as confidently as Hemingway calling for *vin ordinaire* at the Closerie des Lilas. Once, I came down with a violent stomach flu while my mother and I were having lunch in Rene's front window, as we did every two weeks or so. I had absolutely no warning at all, no cramps, no twinges of mild nausea. One minute I was fine, and the next, fluorescent purple vomit was spewing every which way, all over our checkered tablecloth, the potato chips, me. As my mother frantically swabbed the front of my cardigan with insubstantial paper napkins and the staff came running with buckets and mop, I lifted the can to my lips, oblivious to the surrounding patrons' distress, happy there was still plenty left in the can. In my own mind, I continued to cut quite a sophisticated figure.

Rene's vibe was a bit too left-of-mainstream for my grandparents' taste. Their eatery of choice was Laughner's—an enormous faux-colonial cafeteria with plenty of parking just three blocks from their house. We timed it so we'd arrive well in advance of sunset, as did hordes of other senior citizens sharing my grandfather's foresight. No matter how early we got there, it seemed we always got stuck in the back of the line, forced to inch our way along the long hallway leading to the steam tables. Other youngsters passed the time by engaging in mortal combat with their siblings, but I had to content myself with the windows, whose panes bore a harlequin pattern of colored glass. Even this skimpy pleasure involved a wait, as there were only three windows, evenly spaced along the corridor.

"Yessirree, not long now," my grandfather whistled through his teeth, the change jingling in his pocket while I silently counted the heads remaining between me and Window Number Two. "Oh boy-zee, I sure hope they saved us a slice of that chocolate meringue pie!" This was a hell worse than sitting through church. Just when I thought I could stand it no longer, the line would shift, and for a precious minute or two I could plaster my nose to the various colored panes. *This is how the world would look if everything were blue,* I'd think, before moving down a pane. *This is how it'd look if everything were red. What if there was a giant earthquake or something and I got trapped in Laughner's and instead of TV all I had was this window? What if I woke up one morning and everything was yellow, even me?* I prayed that I'd make it to the safe-sized hopper of trays and flatware before any such *Planet of the Apes* scenario could come to pass.

The stout, gray-bunned workers nestling relish plates and monkey dishes into the banked ice at Laughner's salad station seemed an entirely different species from Rene's leotard-topped, hoop-earringed (and, quite possibly, French!) waitresses. *The Stepford Wives* had been judged way too "mature" for a sheltered youngster like me, but the film's television commercial had freaked me out to the point where I began to suspect that the ladies behind the counter might be clones of Gran-Gran's bridge club, pressed into cheerful indentured servitude. They wore black uniforms accessorized with frilly aprons and caps and frequently mistook me for a boy after my mother, in a move no amount of orange pop could make right, authorized her hairdresser to give me a pixie. "White meat or dark, young man?" they'd ask, tongs poised above the stainless steel trough of fried chicken that a middle-aged black man in a fluted paper toque replenished at regular intervals.

"Drumstick, please," I'd whisper.

"Don't let it touch the mashed potatoes," my mother would mouth, as Grampy joyfully announced that he'd spotted vast quantities of pie dead ahead.

"Your grandson has such nice manners," the chicken lady would compliment Gran, handing my dinner across on a special, red-rimmed child's plate decorated with pictures of toys whose popularity had peaked fifty years earlier. Later, when we were seated under the murky oil painting of long-haired kittens that alone distinguished my favorite table, my grandfather would whistle in envy. "Gee whiz, sure wish I could get me one of those special plates," he'd boo-hoo.

Back when I was still young enough for a bridge-club clone to escort us into the dining area, bearing the tray I was incapable of managing myself, Grampy's frustrated desire for a fancy plate brought me close to tears. It killed me to think of him being denied something he wanted so badly. "Maybe next time, if you ask, they'll give you one," I'd say, my chin starting to pucker.

"Robert," Gran-Gran would put in, "'tisn't nice to tease."

"Or I could trade you mine . . ."

"That's okay, honey," Grampy would chuckle, shoveling up some more grayish-brown green beans. "As long as you got one, that's all that really matters. Yessir, we love Laughner's! It's fun-sy!"

Talk about an emotional roller coaster.

"Don't forget your chicken hole," Gran would remind me. "Go on now. Fill it up so we can see all those pretty pictures."

"Can I have a pencil first?" I sniveled. Gran-Gran dug obediently in her pocketbook as, without a word, Mom passed me a suggestion card from the rack provided on every table. As soon as I could read and write, the adults allowed me to provide feedback on behalf of our group, a responsibility I tackled with great seriousness. I collected data and agonized over the gray area between "excellent" and "very good," intent that the ratings I assigned to the pie, the mashed potatoes, and the cleanliness of the dining area should accurately reflect our Laughner's experience.

As the years passed, however, the call of duty was trumped by anarchy's siren song. *Baked beans tasted barfy!* I scrawled, smiling at the inventiveness of my own cruel wit. *I demand a refund!*

"Now, now," Gran frowned, her disapproval, as ever, spurring me on to greater impertinence.

Down with chocolit milk! Up with grape Fanta!

Meatloaf very unsatisfactory. PS—I put it in a doggy bag and my dog thinks so too.

Most of my criticisms were flights of fancy, but my masterpiece, the one that incidentally ended my suggestion-making career, was inspired by an actual event.

I dropped some red Jell-O on the floor. Try and find it.

A few nights later, the phone rang after dinner. "I'll get it! I'll get it!" I screeched from the second floor, racing down the stairs and shoving past my mother, who was loading the dishwasher not two feet from the wall-mounted telephone. What a monster my parents had created when they gave me clearance to start picking up the receiver with a prissy "Halliday residence."

"Miss Halliday?" a deep voice asked.

"Y-yes?" I stammered, wondering what on earth a grown man could possibly want with a kid like me. Was this some fiber-optic version of being pulled into a stranger's car?

"This is Charles Laughner." As in *the* Charles Laughner, the founder whose imposing, gilt-framed portrait hung not far from the suggestion box in the lobby, the evil puppet-master who had cloned all those nice bridge-club ladies! My tongue turned to felt. I gripped the counter with my free hand as my knees started to buckle. "We found your Jell-O." My mother laughed so hard she nearly dropped a piece of Blue Willow.

Good one, Grampy.

The red Jell-O affair ushered in the period in which my affection for Laughner's children's plates went into a lethal tailspin. No self-respecting twelve-year-old wants to eat off something festooned with hobby horses, wagons, and pull toys shaped like duckies, but the bespectacled bridge players who had once taken me for male (despite the flowers embroidered on my overalls) must have missed that memo. The shame of getting saddled with a kiddie plate was intense, but as playground interactions and the fate of Lyman the Green Booger Boy demonstrated, objecting to infantilization often got the protester labeled an even bigger baby. "Looks like somebody's getting a bit too big for her britches," I could imagine a loud-mouthed bridge player remarking, should I hold out for less demeaning crockery. "Somebody's certainly throwing a fuss."

"Uh, drumstick, please," I'd mutter, reaching behind the curtains of long hair shrouding my face to twiddle the studs in my newly pierced ears. Were they so blind to my new status? I was wearing a bra, for god's sake.

"You can give it to her on a regular plate," Mom would interject, in a show of solidarity that demonstrates just how little dignity this world accords seventh graders.

Ultimately, my wish to pass myself off as a person of consequence and maturity in restaurants opened me up to dainties I surely would have refused on home turf. Kiddie menus listed bland items geared toward palates like mine, but too often the reliable standards therein had been given mortifying new names I was loath to pronounce aloud. In order be taken seriously, I would have to confine myself to menus that didn't automatically come with a four-pack of crayons.

With this goal in mind, French onion soup began to seem less a foul broth of dead worms than the type of thing one should order in the stunningly louche, faux-Tiffany-shaded atmosphere of Houlihan's, a chain that caused quite a stir when it opened a franchise around the corner from Florsheim Shoes in the Glendale Mall. The waiter handled the soup gingerly, warning me, as he would anyone, not just a child, to exercise caution around the broiling hot crock. I was relieved to discover that French onion soup came with a thick sedimentary layer of melted cheese, which, though stinky, was also perfectly suited to my purposes, in that eating it involved so much elongating, bundling, and blowing, it saved me from having to confront the titular ingredient. I really thought that was as far as I'd ever be tempted to go. How was I to know that in this context melted cheese is a gateway? That it was only a matter of time until I'd be slamming down the mummy-colored onions lurking like eels beneath the bouillon-soaked bread?

Actually, there were a lot of gateways: the complimentary paper-wrapped sugar cubes that I took the liberty of considering appetizers at the Magic Pan, the rumor that the kerchiefed young employees of Brother Juniper's belonged to a cult, and the old-fashioned telephones Max and Erma's had installed on their conspicuously numbered tables in an effort to attract singles on the make. This was sexy stuff, light-years away from the Li'l Cowpoke's Hot Diggity Dawg mentality from which I sought to disassociate myself. The hostility with which I approached unfamiliar food did not taint my fervor for dining outside the domestic sphere, where well-established routine bowed to the unexpected and the exotic. I might have sung in St. Paul's Episcopal choir, but my tastes were decidedly Catholic. The embroidered Mexican dresses the hostesses wore at Chi-Chi's, the Old Spaghetti Factory's deliberately industrial vibe, the unctuousness of tuxedoed waiters in places where my grandmother

Missy's new husband treated—I was down with them all. What was wrong with my family that they didn't want to eat out every night? When I grew up, I was going to move to New York City and become a famous actress, an occupation where restaurant meals were as much a part of the territory as gorgeous gowns and handsome strangers waiting outside the dressing room with roses. I began to take a greater interest in the cartoons in Grampy's *New Yorker* magazines, which were both incomprehensible and frequently set in restaurants. I might not have gotten the joke, but looking at those cartoons, I knew that I was really looking into a crystal ball, getting a glimpse of my glorious future.

And then my mother recalibrated my coordinates in ways neither of us could have foretold by taking me to the first genuinely ethnic ethnic restaurant of my life. We must have passed the Parthenon dozens of times on our way to Rene's, but it had failed to register, possibly because no éclairs were visible through its window. Inside, it smelled like someone had tried to put a fire out with vinegar. The decorator had evidently called it a day after nailing a dress on the wall. The waiter rested against the back wall smoking a cigarette. I was unsure what to make of a scene that seemed to exist so far outside of my reference level. It sure as hell wasn't French. I had this vague notion that it might be Serbian, a word I must have absorbed subconsciously in geography class, when my waking mind was otherwise occupied passing notes with my immediate neighbors.

The menu in this place might as well have been written in hieroglyphs. Moussaka. Dolma. *What the hell?* Mom was trying to talk me into something called spanakopita. "Ooh, it's yummy," she alleged, as if I could be hooked by a children's menu superlative. I crossed my arms, stonewalling for a more concrete and thus adult description. "Well, it's sort of like a popover," she elaborated. "I get them sometimes at that little grocery stall in the City Market, the one that's right around the corner from Libby's."

Invoking the deli where we went whenever my visits to her workplace coincided with lunchtime was a brilliant move. Not only did their broiled hot dogs' delectably crisp skin go a long way toward healing the psychic wounds inflicted by the water-logged, pantyhose-colored night crawlers she fixed at home, but the place was a magnet for local celebrities. It was impossible to get through lunch there without getting an eyeful of Mayor Hudnut or an anchorman standing at the counter with the rest of the rabble, laying waste to some pastrami with pickle, chips, and a Coke. I got to drink Coke there, too, from waxed paper cups that made it extra delicious. There was a populist feel to the turn-of-the-century market building's open plan that really revved me up. I liked being able to take in all the other stands' sights and smells from Libby's central location. I liked it that mezzanine-level shoppers could look down and see me having lunch with the mayor. I liked it so much that I decided to live on the edge and order what my mother suggested at the Parthenon, the tenuous City Market connection having reassured me that "spanakopita" was probably not Serbian for "Li'l Cowpoke."

The flaky pastries the mustachioed waiter set down in front of us could indeed have passed for popovers, though no cherries oozed out when I cut mine with the side of my fork. "What is this?" I asked, gingerly drawing some of the filling out for a better look.

"That's feta cheese," Mom parried quickly. "Not cottage cheese."

"But what's this other stuff?" I pressed. "The green stuff."

Had Gran been there, she would have made some allusion to Popeye, a tic that only served to deepen my loathing of the mutant-forearmed sailor man. No cartoon character could have induced me to choke down so much as a mouthful of the throat-closing, boiled slime-wads she persisted in serving in a fancy bone-china dish, despite my deep-seated aversion. Daddy, had he been present, would have seized the opportunity to bring up the punch line of his favorite *New Yorker* cartoon: *I say it's spinach and I say the hell with it.*

My mother merely rolled her eyes. Battle fatigue had undermined her decade-plus struggle to get me to eat that which I was determined to hate. "All right," she sighed, "just take a 'courtesy bite.'" I rued the day my parents discovered the vocabulary that went along with Park Tudor's depraved lunchtime policy. They'd been using it against me ever since. A good showing at fruit cocktail was no longer sufficient to get me off the beef Stroganoff hook. There was no winning this proposition. I knew this mandatory try-a-taste business was less concerned with introducing new flavors than humiliating the enemy. (I've now seen two films where characters were forced to eat dog shit, and both times I thought, *Yup, there's your courtesy bite.)* And really, it was childish, as my mother well knew. Why else would she deliver the totemic words with a bit of smirk, as if she was hoping the Parthenon had a booster seat for me, too?

Humiliate a teenager, would she? All right, lady, if that's your game . . . I stabbed up a defiant forkful, golden shards of phyllo showering down as I brought it to my lips. It had probably been suicide to order something that didn't come with a layer of melted cheese, but this was one of those dignity-over-death situations. What had I just put in my mouth, anyway? I had no idea but—oh. My. God. It was like being reborn, like my first taste of Play-Doh, that most sorely missed of nursery school flavors. It tasted like my fingers after ballet class, the hood strings of my old red parka, all sorts of ancient totems I'd once savored sucking on, and simultaneously, like nothing I'd ever known but something I wanted to keep on my tongue forever. In that moment, some synaptic circuit I would never have suspected myself capable of possessing was completed, the same circuit that would eventually lead me to embrace a panoply of strange, low-budget dishes in kerosene-lit back alleys (and, closer at hand, pierce my ears more times than was standard, adorning the holes with dangly, no-carat baubles that made more racket than the coins encircling a belly dancer's ankles). Not yet fully conscious of what she had wrought, my mother flashed me a triumphant, spinach-flecked smile of collusion, then ordered two plates of baklava.

I wondered if this was something the place near Libby's sold, in addition to my strange new favorite food. "Is it chocolate?" I whispered, as the waiter ducked out of sight.

"No," she whispered back, reaching up to finger the dress on the wall. "It's yummy."

spanakopita

Wash 2 lbs of fresh spinach, or, better yet, skip this odious task by ponying up for baby spinach, which looks so clean, it has to be prewashed, right? (If your culinary efforts are to be shared with someone who's more neurotic than you, say, "Yes, yes," when they ask if you washed the spinach first.)

Put it in a mixing bowl, dump some salt on it, and prepare to scream in pain or don rubber gloves should you have a paper cut.

Give that spinach a lovely exfoliating beauty treatment by rubbing the salt into its leaves. (If you failed to spring for baby spinach, you'll have to tear it into smaller pieces while you do this.) Then rinse the salt off and drain.

Beat 7 eggs in a large mixing bowl. Screw your cholesterol! *Opa!*

Crumble in ½ lb of feta cheese, followed by that salty spinach.

Chop an onion, sauté it in olive oil, and into the bowl with you, my friend.

Season to taste with salt, pepper, and oregano.

This is so good that before you go any further, you really should eat a couple of spoonfuls. Why let a little thing like salmonella keep you from experiencing life to its fullest?

Set up a little spanakopita factory by opening a 1 lb box of phyllo dough and covering it with a damp tea towel.

Next to that, put a small pan in which you've melted a stick of butter. You will also need a pastry brush (or, in a pinch, a paintbrush that you've washed really really well and never used for anything but watercolors, to the best of your knowledge).

Then put out the bowl of spinach goop.

Then a buttered cookie sheet.

Carefully peel up a sheet of phyllo, brush it with melted butter, lay another sheet of phyllo atop it, and replace the tea towel over the unused portion. Fold the buttered sheets into thirds vertically.

Now, put some of the spinach goo on the left half of the uppermost third of your long, skinny, folded-up dough. Grasp the right uppermost corner and fold it down over the spinach like a flap.

Now, fold the flapped-up spinach wad over and over, just like a marine folding the flag, which is how they taught us to do it at Gnaw Bone. After 5 or 6 folds, you'll have a fat triangle that you can brush with butter and put on a buttered cookie sheet.

When you've used up all the dough, or all the spinach, drink the remaining butter and pop your triangles in a 375° oven for 50 minutes.

still time for brownies

Brownies figured prominently freshman year, at least among the girls in my social orbit. We were the designated "nice girls," the ones who got good grades and spoke respectfully to teachers and to each other's parents, if not our own. While other, more popular members of our sex dieted, dated, and got blasted at parties where there was no adult supervision, we spent the night at each other's houses, staying up late to bake brownies in our flannel nightgowns. Licking the mixing bowls, we'd jaw endlessly about the "nice" boys upon whom we had crushes and repeat any sizzling gossip we'd managed to glean concerning the sex lives of fast kids like Tina Tyler and Andy Ayers. We'd contribute big batches to fundraising bake sales, then turn around and spend several dollars procuring the largest and gooiest of our fellow bakers' squares to present to each other like friendship bracelets. We comforted ourselves with brownies when sorrowful, tearfully using our fingers to dig up shapeless globs still warm from the pan. We made them from mixes and from scratch, embellished with nuts and M&Ms, frosted bright green for Saint Patrick's Day and orange for Halloween. And nobody made them better, or more frequently, than Gub-Gub.

Gubby and I had been attending the same birthday parties

for years, but I didn't consider her one of my inner circle until Molly and I passed an idle Saturday afternoon leafing through her old *Doctor Dolittle* pop-up book, assigning nicknames to various schoolmates based on which character they most closely resembled, in spirit if not actual appearance. (God knows what the bad girls were up to that day.) One girl we renamed Polynesia because, like the parrot, she was opinionated and bossy, and another was Jip because she shared certain loyal qualities with Dr. Doolittle's even-keeled dog. We fought each other over the rights to Chee-Chee the chimpanzee. I don't recall which of us won, because Gub-Gub was the only name that stuck, probably because the fit was so perfect. Just like the piglet in *Doctor Dolittle*, our Gub-Gub loved treats and festive occasions. Both were inveterate whiners. Our Gubby was even a trifle on the plump side, though to spare her feelings we insisted we'd matched her up with the pig because of the whining alone.

"Why can't I be Chee-Chee?" she pouted, when we brought the book to school as a visual aid.

"Because you're already Gub-Gub," we explained.

Gub-Gub's situation was a bit unusual, in that when her parents divorced, her mom was the one who moved out, leaving Gubby responsible for planning and executing all meals for a household now numbering four. Gubby also shouldered a heaping helping of the child-rearing duties surrounding her younger sister, Chickie, who at exactly ten years our junior was the kind of kid who gets referred to as "a real handful" in public and something else entirely behind closed doors. I think a cleaning woman came in once a week, but otherwise, Gub seemed pretty much on her own domestically. Her father owned his own company but struck me as more of an absentminded professor type, and her big brother, Pat, was a misanthropic genius given to barricading himself into his room to bone up on the French New Wave, rewrite incredibly dense computer programs, and seethe with resentment toward his sister and all her shallow friends. No wonder poor Gubby whined all the time.

Strangely, she never seemed to resent having to prepare meals, even if their reception was invariably spoiled by one of Chickie's screeching meltdowns or the poisonous presence of silent Pat. She may have whined for the full hour it took to prepare her entrée, but only because that was her standard MO. Cooking went to her head the way the smell of theatrical pancake makeup went to mine. The average teenage girl in Gubby's situation might be tempted to follow my father's culinary example, but this girl was cut from different cloth, i.e., the same cloth as my mother. The two of them used to do postmortems of *Gourmet* while I skulked in the shadows like chopped liver. "Did you see that Dijon chicken baked with apples?" Gubby would ask, sending Mom riffling through the latest issue in hot pursuit. "Keep going. It's past the asparagus."

"What, this one? I don't know, seems like an awful lot of thyme to me."

"Do you think so?" Frowning, Gubby leaned over to scrutinize the magazine in my mother's lap. "Hmm."

"You could try rosemary," my mother mused.

"Oh, yes, that would be much, much better," Gubby cried

happily, as if she could taste the difference, and indeed, I think she could. It was all just Simon and Garfunkel lyrics to me.

When I went to her house, I invariably wound up on chopping detail, though sometimes, like, say, when Chickie streaked by, nude save for the elf skirt she'd worn in the kindergarten pageant and the Magic Marker war paint she'd scrawled all over her arms and legs, Gubby would have to entrust me with a higher degree of responsibility. "Can you keep an eye on this?" she would ask, gesturing impatiently to a pan of *coq au vin* simmering on the stove. "She can't go to school tomorrow if I don't get her in the tub."

"Wait, what do I do?"

"Oh, you know," she whined, anxious to get going. "Just keep checking it and add some more wine if it looks like it needs it."

"How can I tell if it needs it?"

But she had already rushed upstairs on the heels of her sister, leaving me in charge of the fragrant pan bubbling merrily of its own accord. As nervous as I felt about ruining her family's dinner, I couldn't resist adding a little splash from the bottle she'd left on the counter, to demonstrate that I had a few chops, too.

"Get away from me! I hate you!" I could hear Chickie screaming, somewhere in the upper reaches.

Tentatively, I reached for a small jar marked "bay leaf" and chucked one in. I swore I could detect its flavor in the finished dish.

Like many talented chefs, Gubby had a highly evolved sense of aesthetics, which turned her into a real Veruca Salt regarding flower arrangements and napkin colors, but also made her a lot of fun for an uncoordinated art freak like me to be around, since she enjoyed drawing nearly as much as cooking. Once when I was spending the night at Gubby's, a huge blizzard kicked up, and it took three days before we could dig out enough to get me home. To stave off boredom, we drew elaborate cartoons of our idealized future selves, complete with flattering outfits and devoted husbands culled from the ranks of the boys we knew. We kept our energy up with James Taylor records and four batches of cream cheese frosting, which we spooned like ice cream from cereal bowls. Varying the food coloring with every batch, we ran through a brand-new box of powdered sugar in no time flat. I almost wished the snow would never melt.

My friends and I entered high school already heavily influenced by *Seventeen* magazine. By the middle of seventh grade, the Flame Glow cosmetics, Bobbie Brooks casual wear, Sea Breeze astringent, Noxzema medicated skin cream, Tickle antiperspirant, Nadine formals, and Love's Baby Soft cologne advertised in its pages had supplanted the FAO Schwarz catalogue's puppet theaters and fairy costumes as objects of near-supernatural wonderfulness. The editorial content, with its emphasis on nifty holiday gift ideas and homemade complexion scrubs purportedly used by the models, spoke to "nice girls" in a way *Tiger Beat*'s semisleazy pullout posters of teen heartthrobs like Scott Baio and Rex Smith did not.

Biding my time in the purgatory of junior high, I savored the annual prom-centric March issue, yearning for the corsages, dates, and specialty lingerie *Seventeen* posited as such sacred components of life to come. It killed me that the beauty editor repeatedly decreed bangs the hairstyle best suited to my high forehead. I didn't want bangs. I wanted to be like Phoebe Cates, *Seventeen*'s most beautiful and frequent cover girl, whose Indian princess hair and doe eyes beat the pants off the all-American sportiness of Tara and Tracy, the sun-kissed, spiral-maned twins.

Phoebe's seminal contribution to a December feature on models' favorite holiday memories concerned a Christmas morning she and her sister had spent in bed, eating leftover Chinese food straight from the carton, an image of such towering exoticism and emancipation, I nearly hyperventilated. I was no less enamored of the regular teen activities in which Phoebe was shown taking active part, skipping up the library steps toward mixed-gender study dates, building perfect snowmen on blanketed winter football fields, flaunting doily-trimmed hearts from secret Valentines, welcoming spring by bottle-feeding a newborn lamb, making her own potpourri, and looking fucking awesome in a white bikini.

About midway through freshman year, I accepted that my experience was never going to mirror hers. The fantasy hayrides, ice-skating dates, tree-trimming get-togethers, make-your-own-sundae parties, south-of-the-border fiestas, graduation brunches, and Fourth of July cookouts I'd been led to expect gave way to the dismal reality of bimonthly dances in the Commons, where the boys spent the fast songs slouched against the wall and the slow songs frenching the likes of Tina Tyler.

One staple of high school that *Seventeen* never sought to depict was the unchaperoned blowout. My ears pricked up every time Lissa Lucas stomped through the Monday morning halls, screeching endless variations of, "You guys, I was so wasted, I totally puked in Skid's Camaro!" In truth, I'd have eaten tacks to attend one of these bashes, but even an offhanded invitation seemed unlikely when the in-crowders I'd known since grade school stared right through me as if I were just so much ecto-plasm, fiddling with the combination of a locker next to theirs. Between the two fantasies, *Seventeen* and the vomit-splattered Camaro, that riverside picnic in the July issue was the hands-down winner. Phoebe and her friends got there on three-speed bikes, which they pedaled down a country lane, one of the twins wearing a cylindrical basket of baguettes strapped photogenically across her back.

The high school events *Seventeen* had insisted we'd treasure forever turned out to be no match for the dark forces of Lissa Lucas and Tina Tyler. Even if the whole pack of them had been suspended en masse the day before some big to-do, the boys with whom we wanted to associate had proven themselves incapable of any initiative beyond propping up the walls and calling each other by their last names. Our best hope of wooing them was to feed them in settings and groupings large enough to fool them into thinking our designs were purely platonic—in other words, picnics. They wouldn't have to dance. They wouldn't have to put themselves through the agony of asking anyone for a date. If they were at a loss for words, they wouldn't lack for something to occupy their mouths. No other extracurricular activity seemed as easy to control, especially with Gub-Gub, the biggest control freak of us all, calling the shots.

She insisted on chocolate-dipped strawberries, pretty

napkins, and bona fide baskets. If one of us toted the lemonade jug to the prearranged site in a plastic bag, Gubby would promptly shove it underneath the blanket so it wouldn't show up in the pictures. The food on these outings was plentiful, labor-intensive, and, above all, "special." Left to my own devices, I might have been content to loll directly on the grass with a bag of my grandmother's chocolate chip cookies, some dried beef, and a can of Dr. Pepper, but such a tawdry display could never have passed muster with Miss Gubby, whose manifesto for these productions was the *The Silver Palate Cookbook*, a volume so catering to her strengths and obsessions, I was amazed she hadn't authored it herself.

In lieu of photos, whimsical line drawings accompanied recipes for Linzer Hearts, Miniature Chevre Tarts, and Glazed Blueberry Chicken. Quotes from the likes of *Eloise* and *Alice in Wonderland* peppered the margins, as did suggested menus in celebration of New Year's Eve, the Academy Awards, May Day, the vernal equinox, and sending one's friends off to Europe. If only the authors had supplied a specific menu for snagging the "nice boys" who followed their stomachs because they were too inhibited to follow their dicks. I felt more than a little impatient with the innocence of their responses to our salad niçoise and red raspberry pie. After a post–sophomore year, summerlong liaison with a strange and sardonic older boy, who was, awkwardly enough, Gubby's brother Pat's best friend, I'd come to hope for something more than just compliance on the boys' end.

Sadly, it seemed the only thing these preppies were horny for was second, and possibly third, helpings. We girls prepared the lushest, creamiest chicken salads in the book, and still, relations among our set remained tragically chaste. The only one to find herself a bona fide nice-boy boyfriend was Molly, and she couldn't cook. Still, Gubby and I hauled roquefort, seedless grapes, and cold primavera to the grounds of the art museum, Butler University's formal Holcomb Gardens, and every other pastoral setting between Carmel and Zionsville. The boys got it up to make fun of the napkins Gubby had selected with such care, but that was all. Not only were these preppies incapable of recognizing apple-and-walnut salad as the first move we so clearly intended it to be, they were paralyzed when it came to making the second. Then one of them discovered vodka. Fucking *finally*.

This liquid miracle came about when one of our peers, a gawky outsider whose patchwork madras pants made him an object of derision even at the height of the *Preppy Handbook* craze, underwent a Cinderella-like transformation. Almost overnight, Philip became known as Boney, the mastermind behind the instantaneously legendary, abundantly stocked weekly bashes that started shortly after school every Friday and raged until the wee hours of Sunday morning. The nickname was bestowed by none other than Skid, the popular, hard-partying linebacker, owner of the fabled Camaro. Philip had been a disaster, but Boney, the outrageous junior boozehound in the crazy madras pants, was the host with the most, which, as Lemony Snicket might say, means a rec room, a pool table, a television permanently tuned to the fledgling MTV, and a mother who didn't seem to give a damn that a hundred kids showed up every weekend to get screaming drunk.

In his previous incarnation, Boney had played on the golf and tennis teams with some of our nice boys, so there was no need to prevaricate when our parents asked where we were headed on Saturday nights. To their way of thinking, he was of a piece with the young men wolfing down their daughters' new-potato salad with mustard and dill. We girls had never placed him in that category, of course, never envisioned him coming along on Gubby's gorgeously orchestrated picnics. Before his transformation, he was too laughable, and after, too fabulously, self-consciously famous, prancing across the baize of his late father's much-abused pool table, waving a box of Wheat Thins around in a pitch-perfect imitation of Sandy Duncan.

Just like Gub-Gub, Boney lived for things to be special. Once he snuck off campus during lunch period to plug a bottle of grain alcohol into a twenty-pound watermelon he was serving later that night. His sense of festivity was suspiciously, deliciously girlish. If the legal drinking age had been lowered to fifteen, *Seventeen* would have loved this guy. His sexual preference was anyone's guess, but he never shied from participation. The homecoming float was built in his garage. He chaired the carnation sale. He was religious in his attendance at such official extracurricular events as the fall musical, the spring concert, and the senior luau, rolling up in the white Cadillac convertible he'd inherited from his grandmother and equipped with a portable bar. When Christmas came around, he presented even his least personal lady friends with red moiré sachets shaped like teddy bears. He was no one's boyfriend, but he made me feel like Phoebe Cates.

By the middle of senior year, I had managed to get myself seriously involved with a nice boy. James was reticent, undemonstrative, and fairly temperate at Boney's, annoying me by refusing to play F. Scott to my Zelda, no matter how much gin I sloshed down my throat sans mixer or even glass. Still, I was crazy about him, this slender, inoffensive fellow upon whom the many feelings I'd been waiting to lavish on someone could be lavished, if not precisely reciprocated in the grand style I would have preferred. My mother approved of him wholeheartedly. How could she not? He was Timothy Hutton in *Ordinary People*, minus the crazy, tormented, passionate, suicidal parts.

"Why don't you invite James and some of your other friends over for dinner before the Valentine's dance?" Mom suggested out of the blue. As the mother of an only child, she'd always seemed unnerved by the prospect of having more than two teenagers in the house at one time, particularly if they were of mixed gender. Now, without warning, she was behaving like that big softie who ran the soda fountain frequented by the *Happy Days* gang. "Is Molly still hot and heavy with Sam?"

"Uh, yeah," I said cautiously. Her frank, friendly interest left me as aghast as if I'd been busted in the backseat with my pants off. Had aliens been probing her, or was this the punishment for having a boyfriend my mother seemed to like as much as I did, albeit in a much more virginal way? I was used to the subject of teen romance making her discernibly uncomfortable. Now she wanted in?

"Who's Marybeth taking?" she continued in a breezy, chummy tone that she seemed to feel was in keeping with the Sadie Hawkins nature of the impending affair.

"God, Mom. Devin! She's been going with him since September."

"Oh, he's such a nice boy." My ass. She should have scratched a little deeper than his upstanding parents and his preppy clothes. "How about poor old Gubby?"

"What do you mean 'poor old Gubby'?"

"Well, I just feel bad that she doesn't have anyone special the way the rest of you—"

"Mom! Stop feeling sorry for her! She's fine! She doesn't want your pity!" My overreaction owed less to the tense nature of this highly unusual situation than to the uncomfortable sensation that I, myself, was doing unto Gubby as Molly had done unto me back when she'd landed her man. We'd even had a little falling-out about it, a two-month standoff that ended with a bouquet of irises and a plate of blondies left on my doorstep.

"Is she taking anyone to the dance?" my mother pressed, so delicately she might have been asking how the chemo was going.

"Yes! Michael! Okay?!"

"Oh, Michael Corliss. I always thought he was such a nice boy." If I heard the phrase "nice boy" applied as a superlative one more time, I was going to scream. Seething, I yanked the Saran Wrap off a plate of leftover lemon squares and crammed one in, whole. Parental approval can be a terrible thing. "So, old Gubby's finally laid aside her torch for Eric?" Mom snickered. Gubby's unrequited crush on Eric Heyl had such an epic quality that even my mother had incontrovertible proof of it. It could be traced back to fifth grade without so much as a single flicker of interest on Eric's part (though of course this coldness had been edited out when we spent the blizzard drawing him as Gubby's husband in our future cartoons).

"Eric's going with some girl from North Central." I muttered, stacking a handful of lemon squares on a paper napkin in advance of my escape. "And Gubby and Michael are just going as friends, so don't blow it all out of proportion, because she's not. It's not a real date."

"Well, if you and Gubby would like to have your dates and a few other couples over for refreshments beforehand, I'd be happy to contribute some lemon squares, or whatever you'd like," she reiterated in a slightly less chipper tone.

I felt torn. There was not a doubt in my mind that Boney, in addition to his traditional post-dance blowout, would be hosting an informal open house for anyone wishing to get fully tanked before braving the confines of the balloon-embellished gym. On the other hand, Gubby's escort, Michael, didn't drink anything stronger than Mountain Dew, a wrinkle she hoped I would take into account on her behalf. "Please," she wheedled, when I presented Mom's idea to her as something no one in her right mind would want to do. "I don't want to get stuck being the only one who isn't going to Boney's because her stupid date doesn't drink!"

"Yeah, but it'd just be you and me and Marybeth."

"Oh, do Molly and Sam want to do something 'private'?" she sneered. Good old Gubby. She always knew just the right moment to mock my semi-estranged former best friend.

"No, they're going to Boney's." It bothered me that Molly and Sam numbered among Boney's inner circle, invited to dine with him and his mother, whereas I was just one of dozens of girls, scrambling on top of the pool table to swing a cue around samurai style whenever the VJ introduced the Vapors' "Turning Japanese" video, which was, like, approximately once an hour.

"Swear that you guys won't abandon me with Michael so you can go to Boney's! Please?" she beseeched. "Pretty please with sugar on top? Can't we do your mom's idea? It doesn't have to be dinner! We could make dessert. A whole bunch of desserts! Ooh, I know, a dessert buffet!" Pressing her palms together beneath her chin, she awaited my answer with an imploring and terribly hopeful gaze. Maybe I could have said no when all I'd have been denying her was the pleasure of my company, but now that she'd brought the dessert buffet into the mix, there was no way. It would be like tearing up her *Silver Palate* and throwing it in her face.

"Oh my god, that's so *Seventeen* I could gag," I said, grudgingly nodding my assent.

I had expected that Gubby would have settled on a menu of Viennese splendor well in advance of the pending event, but she seemed blithely unconcerned. Perhaps pairing with Michael, whom we'd both known since childhood, removed some of the impetus to go chasing after scrumptious new confections for this event, the way she would have had she, by some miracle, found herself cooking for Eric Heyl. She had several oft-baked recipes for various species of brownies that I figured would do just fine if she wasn't moved to attempt something special. "I'll just come over to your house in the morning, and we can go to the grocery after we figure out what to make," she said. "What are you going to wear?"

"You know that Victorian-looking blouse? I was thinking maybe that with those hot pink pants, the ones that start out baggy and then get tight around the ankles."

"Ooh, that sounds Valentiney."

"What are you wearing, Gubby?" She had recently managed to shed a noticeable amount of weight, through a combination of lap swimming and staunch resistance in the face of cream-cheese frosting. She'd celebrated by running up her father's credit cards on a staggering array of new finery, most of which she schlepped to my house in an enormous duffel bag on the day of the dance. Laura Ashley led the pack, but there were also several dressy skirts and romantic, lace-collared blouses among the contenders. Five pairs of loafers and Pappagallos were unpacked for my review. She'd brought enough makeup to open her own department store counter, but as she pointed out, her blush, eye shadow, and lip gloss palette depended on whatever ensemble she ended up wearing. Declaring that the add-a-pearl necklace her father had given her when she was a baby "bit penie," she fell to rummaging in my jewelry box.

"Girls? Have you decided what you're making?" my mother called upstairs.

We were still deciding, we called back.

Forty-five minutes later, she offered to preheat the oven.

We told her to cool her jets.

"Your guests will be arriving shortly!" she barked a bit later. "Shall I set out some bread and water?" My mother has never had much tolerance for leaving things to chance. She'd been quite keen when informed of the dessert buffet angle, so much so that every minute we spent holed up in my room seemed to grate on her, as if our appearance was of little import compared to the evening's real purpose. I wondered if she thought I was hogging my friend all to myself.

"She's getting pissed," I said.

"And now it's too late for Chocolate Decadence," Gubby whimpered, a rueful expression on her face.

"We could just make brownies."

"Yes, but brownies aren't special!"

"Girls!" my mother shouted. "Come see! I think I may have stumbled onto a solution!"

"Solution to what?" Gubby mouthed as we clattered down the stairs. Mom was waiting for us at the foot, a cast-iron pan of some sort held aloft like the Statue of Liberty's beacon. Nobody said anything for a second or two. I was unclear what was expected of us, but the ball seemed to be in our court.

"Um, do you know how much butter you have?" Gub ventured, timidly. "Because there's a recipe for shortbread—"

"Heart. Shaped. Waffles," my mother announced, overriding Gubby with a mad gleam in her eye. "Could we come up with anything more perfect if we tried? Heart-shaped waffles for Valentine's Day." Gubby bit her lip dubiously but was too polite to say anything.

"I don't like maple syrup," I reminded my mother.

"Maple syrup?" Mom scoffed. "Pooh! I'm not talking about breakfast! These are heart-shaped dessert waffles, to be served with powdered sugar or jam or individual bowls of dipping sauce!"

"Ooh, we could make a lovely raspberry one!" Gubby cried, snapping back into character so quickly, it was as if the fashion parade upstairs had been her Oz, the fantastic result of a mild concussion.

"Raspberry, or maybe some sort of sweetened cream cheese," my mother agreed.

"Won't it be hard to control the batter, though?" Gubby worried. "So that the waffles come out looking like hearts?"

"That," Mom answered, throwing her shoulders back dramatically, "is the beauty of my heart-shaped waffle iron!" She unhinged the pan she'd been holding to reveal cast-iron, mirror-image flowers whose petals were, indeed, heart shaped. "Art gave it to me four Christmases ago, but I've never had occasion to use it until now."

"Oh, Ayunee, let's!" Gubby squealed, seizing my arm. I glanced at the old-school house clock hanging by the stove. Molly and Sam were probably already over at Boney's, clinking glasses with his mother in the first, ceremonial drink of the evening. If we went to the grocery now, we'd barely have time to put on our makeup before Marybeth and the boys arrived.

"You girls go take your showers or whatever it is you do to make yourselves presentable," my mother ordered, pulling eggs and milk from the fridge with military precision. "I'll get the waffle operation started, so that once you're dressed, you can concentrate on the dipping sauces."

"Oh, shit!" came the muffled hiss. The heating register cut directly into the floor of my bedroom conducted every sound originating in the kitchen below, and the clatter that had started when I headed off to the shower had escalated steadily, though not, it seemed, happily. School might have been the provenance of R-rated profanity, but we "nice girls" rarely heard it at home. My stepfather's language could get pretty raw, but the only time my mother let loose with something stronger than "hell" or "damn" was in the hours leading up to her annual New Year's Day open house, when the stress of entertaining sent her into such a state that Art and I instinctively scuttled in different directions, lest she smite us with her electric egg-beater. The kitchen sounds now floating up through my register were giving me a bad auld lang syne feeling.

There was a brief lull and then, "Shit, shit, shit!" Gubby and I exchanged worried glances over our mascara wands.

"Oh, for Christ's sake, you fu—" The rest of the exclamation was obscured by the harsh report of metal striking metal.

"I think your mother just said the F-word," Gubby whispered, clutching a frilly white blouse to her chest.

"Happy Valentine's Day," I whispered back grimly, lifting my hair so she could fasten the clasp of my heart-shaped pendant. Anything to delay boarding the *Hindenburg.*

"Girls!" My mother screeched, as if she could hear us too. "Get dressed and get down here! Now!"

"Better hurry," I whispered as Gubby reached into the depths of the duffel bag, searching for another, previously rejected blouse. "Come on, it's just Michael. It's not like you're going with Eric."

The scene greeting us at the foot of the stairs this time was decidedly unpropitious, especially with half an hour left until our guests were due to arrive. Mom, her hair frizzed from the heat of the burners, whipped around to face us with the demonic, bug-eyed intensity of a "Big Daddy" Roth hot-rodder. The tattered remains of torn waffle hearts lay heaped on every available surface. Under the circumstances, it seemed like the best course of action would be to head the others off at the front porch. "These little sons-of-bitches refuse to unweld themselves from the pan," Mom spat, hurling the butter knife she'd been using like a crowbar into the sink. Christ, she'd sailed clear around the

Horn this time. "This is what I've been contending with while you girls were upstairs, making yourselves 'beautiful.'"

"We've still got time for brownies," I suggested.

"Oh no!" she threatened, looking like she was about to yank the delicate filigree heart earrings she'd given me straight down the middle of my lobes. "Nobody's switching horses in mid-stream! Not at this stage of the game! You wanted heart-shaped waffles, so let's just try to see if we can't make that happen!" *Oh, sweet lord, no.* Why on earth had I agreed to this? I could have been halfway through my second gin and Sprite at Boney's, lounging on the pool table while Devo and Duran Duran mixed it up on MTV.

"Have you tried greasing the surface with Pam?" Gubby asked, nudging me aside to join my mother at the stove. Was she off her rocker? Gubby was a good cook and all, but she had overstepped her bounds on this one. Her timing couldn't have been worse. Didn't she know better than to dick around inside a lion's cage, particularly when that lion was in a New Year's Day mood? I braced myself for Mom to rip her head off, but instead she hesitated, apparently bewildered by the mention of nonstick cooking spray. It almost looked as if she didn't know where she was. Then, to my shock, she held up a stick of butter.

As gently as a hostage negotiator persuading a psycho to surrender her weapon, Gubby took the butter and set it on top of the refrigerator. "Or if you don't have any Pam, maybe vegetable oil," she suggested soothingly, with a level of patience and empathy rarely on display when she was wrestling Chickie into a pair of clean tights. "Do you have anything we could use as a spatula besides that knife?" As I gaped in disbelief, my mother mutely permitted Gub-Gub to swab the iron with Wesson, then ladle a portion of batter over the gleaming treads. She closed the hatch and then we waited. The schoolhouse clock's pendulum echoed in the otherwise empty house. My stepfather had wisely absented himself, saying he had "no interest in a bunch of high school kid shit."

"Six fifteen," I observed, just to feel like I was doing something useful. Dollars to doughnuts, Phoebe Cates had never fallen victim to this kind of catastrophic hubris. Just as in the *Peanuts* Christmas special, *Seventeen*'s staged festivities relegated parents to a strictly offstage role.

Suddenly, Mom let out a happy cry as Gub-Gub coaxed a perfectly browned waffle flower from the iron onto one of our Blue Willow plates, then delicately tugged at the petals, separating them into five distinct hearts. I had abandoned hope that such a miracle could come to pass. The demon who'd possessed my mother immediately relinquished his claim, banished until New Year's. "Three cheers for Gubby!" she declared. "Gubby saves the day!"

"What about the sauces?" Gub-Gub asked, brushing off the kudos as she prepared the iron for the next five petals. "It won't be nearly so good if we don't have lots of little bowls to choose from."

Elsewhere in Indianapolis, teenagers were ordering pizza and getting drunk.

"I'll go get the peanut butter," I mumbled, praying that maybe between *Seventeen* and *The Silver Palate*, some of Gub-Gub's magic would have rubbed off on me. "And whatever else I can find."

gub–gub brownies

Preheat oven to 350°.

Melt 2 sticks of butter. Sweet Jesus.

Then add 2 cups of brown sugar, 2 eggs, and 2 teaspoons of vanilla.

Better taste some to make sure nobody poisoned it.

Thank god you're still alive to add 1½ cups of flour, 2 teaspoons of baking powder, and 1 teaspoon of salt.

Discuss boys for 5 or 10 minutes to give the dough a chance to cool off a little.

Add 2 cups of chocolate chips. (But first, as a favor to me, do a little Internet research to see which brand is owned by a conglomerate that gladhands its infant formula to impoverished families in developing countries in order to create "customers" who can ill afford a product they didn't need in the first place and now mix with dirty water. Then buy another brand.)

Don't forget to discuss the boys, though. Remember, the Internet didn't exist when I was in high school. I wouldn't have known an instant message if it bit me in the ass.

Pour in a greased 13" x 9" pan and bake for 30 to 40 minutes.

These suckers have a long shelf life, so mail them to all your friends who have already left for college.

horse chow

My college apartment boasted the biggest kitchen of anyplace I have ever lived, save the fancy dining-roomed brick colonial where, when I was five, I witnessed an Indianapolis veterinarian performing emergency countertop surgery on my cat amid casseroles from the Junior League luncheon raging one room over. My male housemates, Randall and Clyde, viewed the kitchen primarily as a place for stowing their cereal and ramen, which gave me free rein to equip it as I saw fit. With over a dozen cabinets and drawers to fill, this was an almost unbearably thrilling assignment, far more rousing than slogging through the history plays in my *Riverside Shakespeare.*

I'd owned a wok and a fistful of chopsticks since my friend Lisa Hickey introduced me to the art of stir-frying, freshman year. From time to time we liked to bag out on the meal plan for which we had registered at the beginning of the semester, in order to make dinner for ourselves in the roach-infested kitchen tucked behind the reeking common room in my dorm's basement. Few of my fellow residents even knew it existed, which allowed Lisa and me to behave as if it were ours alone, though in observance of Smokey the Bear's rules, we always left it in the same filthy condition in which we'd found it.

Lisa hailed from an entirely different planet than Gub-Gub,

as their approaches to cooking confirmed. Gubby relished complicated recipes, cute oven mitts, dessert, and the sort of table settings one might have encountered dining with Claude Monet in his garden at Giverny. Lisa, who had no sweet tooth but enjoyed licking rice cakes so the extra salt she sprinkled on after every bite would compound, was a much more freewheeling character. Where Gubby measured, Lisa slung. Guided by intuition and the memory of past exploits, she snatched up ingredients I would never have dared to experiment with, as much as I enjoyed them when they turned up in Chinese food.

"Ayunee, these peapods are awesome," she would declare, admiring one in the morgue-like light of the lone fluorescent tube that flickered anemically from the flaking ceiling. She looked like she was about to start meditating on it.

"Am I supposed to leave their legs on?" I asked the first time I was tossed a dripping plastic bag of raw shrimp. Their deathly pallor was impossible to reconcile with the plump, coral-colored specimens I so relished with cocktail sauce.

Her head cocked to one side, Lisa took a sip of the Marlboro Light balanced on her lower lip and considered. As much as she may have envied the seemingly effortless academic abilities I had osmosed through my alma mater's "tradition of excellence," she was the one with real wisdom to impart: smoking, stir-frying, dressing, dancing, interior decorating via cunning use of fringe-edged cotton hippie shawls . . . so what if she was not 100 percent clear on the proper way to clean raw shrimp?

"Yeah, fuck it, we don't need 'em," she decided after a moment's reflection. "I don't want to be crunching through that shit, do you?"

Lisa liked to wait to add soy sauce until the oil in the wok was searing hot, a practice that sent tiny brown speckles flying over everything within a two-foot range and frequently tripped the smoke alarm for the entire dorm. By the time the emergency personnel worked their way down to the basement, in search of a blaze and any residents whom smoke inhalation might have prevented from joining the three hundred others now shivering in the courtyard, we'd be sitting down to dinner at the kitchen's rickety card table. I always felt chastened by the Proper Procedures lecture that followed our discovery, but not Hickey.

"You sure you don't want some?" she'd beam up at an exasperated, middle-aged firefighter wearing twenty-five pounds of gear. "It's awesome."

I brought the wok and chopsticks from my dorm days to the kitchen I was to nominally share with Randall and Clyde. Additionally, I had inherited a large blue platter from Sweden and an orange Le Creuset casserole, both scavenged from my mother's overflowing cabinets. Oh, and I can't forget the ramekins, eight small ones in a red-on-white pattern of dots and bows best suited to little girls' bargain-brand underpants, which Mom had purchased at T. J. Maxx as a housewarming present for my first-ever apartment. "What are they?" I had asked, after thanking her for the gift. "Candy dishes?"

"You don't know what ramekins are?" she had replied, unable to believe that one so tight with Gub-Gub could exist in a state of such ignorance. "Oh, you can use them for anything, really! Chocolate mousse or individual soufflés. . . . " This sounded a little suspect coming from a woman who still made fun of the escargot pans she'd received as a housewarming present seven years earlier.

Gran-Gran, aghast that her oldest granddaughter had scuppered propriety by moving off campus with housemates who could scarcely be described as "nice girls," nonetheless sent a housewarming package of her own. It contained a roll of paper towels, a loaf of banana bread, three dented measuring cups, a fussy double boiler with chickadee decals on the lid, and so many forks I worried that she and Grampy would be eating their pot roast with spoons.

I played with this booty much as I had my childhood dollhouse, arranging and rearranging to my heart's content, laying the groundwork for scenarios in which parties, Christmas, and/or sex could figure predominantly. Just as the tiny Ping-Pong tables and coffee grinders in that to-scale New England Saltbox had fueled the lust to acquire infinitely more miniature accessories, presiding over Mom's and Gran's hand-me-down cookware left me feeling that I didn't have nearly enough. There were things that no self-respecting home chef should do without, I informed Randall and Clyde, who were on the vinyl couch in our dining room savoring their mid-afternoon corn flakes.

"Fine with me, as long as you don't expect us to help you pay for it," Randall said, his hand raised in benediction.

"No, no, of course not, not that it's going to cost much. I'm getting everything at Amvets." This was the charity benefited by the huge, if mildly pestilential, thrift store Hickey had discovered next door to the Steppenwolf Theatre.

"Whatever you get, promise me you'll wash it first," Randall enjoined.

"Randall, of course I'm going to wash it." Impatient to get going, I pulled my paternal grandmother Missy's castoff mink coat on over my striped railroad engineer's overalls.

"Oh, like you washed those ratty old sweaters you and Lisa dragged back from there last week?" He appealed to Clyde with a raised eyebrow.

"Those are different. They're beaded."

"Ayun, please, just promise me that you'll wash them before you put them away."

"Jesus, okay, yes, your majesty, I'll wash them! I'll wash them!"

"With soap and really hot water. Not the way you usually do."

Brimming with resentment, I promised.

"Ooh, and can you see if they have anything that would make a good breastplate?" Clyde called after me. "Kristi and I are doing *Medea* in class on Friday."

My college years coincided with a particularly fertile period in the annals of thrift-store shopping, and Amvets was *la crème.* Not exactly breastplate fertile, but the housewares department spilled forth as if from a particularly bountiful cornucopia, light-years removed from the sparse selection of scratched Teflon, battered plastic, and grimy flesh-colored dish racks that it is today. The wobbly shelving groaned with treasure for an aspirant earth mama raring to feed the multitudes on a meager student's budget.

No longer irritated with Randall and Clyde, thanks to the good vibes emanating from the mounting pile in my shopping cart,

I imagined them sitting around in bathrobes with my boyfriend, Mr. Swain, the most gentlemanly twenty-one-year-old in the history of Northwestern University. How the three of them would enjoy the homemade pancakes I would fry up in this pale blue, enameled skillet, using that wood-handled vintage spatula.

With so many cabinets to fill, I was hard pressed to resist an old-fashioned eggbeater, a Bundt pan, two boxes of Mason jars, and a dozen pie plates embossed with the logos of defunct bakeries. Those raised letters ultimately wreaked havoc on the leaden spinach and wheat-germ crusts I attempted to fashion from *The Enchanted Broccoli Forest*, but even so, I remained a sucker for their charmingly outmoded appearance. Ditto Bromwell's Measuring-Sifter (Pat. No 1,753,995). Wild horses couldn't have stopped me from buying that thing, even though sifting, in a post-Gubby culinary world presided over by Lisa Hickey, seemed the sort of uptight directive one could dispense with, to negligible effect.

Despite Gran's conviction that sex, drugs, and degradation were the only things that could come of my gender-crossing, off-campus household, it turned out that my primary extracurricular activity—after the sex and drugs—was cooking. It was all very wholesome, though the carob, soy milk, lentils, and other communist ingredients filling my pantry would not have seemed so to my Presbyterian grandmother. Most of these goods had been procured under Lisa Hickey's tutelage, using her employee discount at the Oak Street Market, a brightly lit health food store a short bike ride from my apartment. I had heard of health food before arriving at Northwestern. Growing up in the '70s, you couldn't escape at least a passing familiarity with Euell Gibbons, the natural foods advocate and Grape-Nuts spokesman whose name was guaranteed to draw a big laugh in campfire skits, particularly if delivered while pretending to eat a pinecone. But prior to Oak Street, I'd been inside a health food store but once, when my mother took me to buy a pair of genuine Earth Shoes to go with my zip-front corduroy jumpsuit, both of which were de rigueur for sixth-grade girls.

What had struck me immediately was that there were no carts. Of course, there would have been no way to maneuver them through the tiny aisles, up and down the short flights of stairs connecting warrenlike rooms full of dehydrated fruit, dried beans, nuts with the shells still on, bins of spiky dried herbs, and wooden barrels containing every grain on earth save good old Pillsbury Enriched All Purpose Flour. It was like Mrs. Tittlemouse's house, only dusty and much, much bigger. The whole thing seemed slightly shady to me. I mean, what kind of grocery sells shoes? "Would you care for some Purina Horse Chow?" my mother snickered, nudging me as we navigated our way to the back.

Ironically, Horse Chow became one of my favorite things to prepare when at last I was blessed with my very own kitchen. I had unearthed the recipe—a mixture of raw oats, salt, raisins, and olive oil—from a hippie cookbook I checked out of the Evanston Public Library when I decided to bake bread from scratch. The labor-intensive loaf that ended that experiment proved as edible as a doorstop, but Horse Chow was a keeper. To eat it with a wooden spoon, perched before the window in such a way that my long hair was warmed by a shaft of sunlight in which dust motes twirled like teeny ballerinas, seemed a better sacrament than any I'd experienced in the Episcopal church.

"You know, they make instant oatmeal," Randall scoffed, his scrawny shoulders shuddering beneath the bright purple fleece of his official Northwestern sweatshirt. "It comes in individual serving packets. All you do is add boiling water."

"And it comes in all sorts of neat flavors," Clyde added as he stuffed a sleeveless unitard, a banana, and the script of *Barefoot in the Park* into his gym bag.

"That's right," Randall said. "Maple and Brown Sugar, Strawberries 'n' Cream—"

"Apple Shhinnammon!" Clyde interrupted in the obnoxious Carol Channing voice he'd taken to using with such frequency that eventually, Randall and I would have no recourse but to place a classified ad in the *Daily Northwestern*, seeking a new housemate.

Horse Chow was the least ambitious dish to come out of that big kitchen while I sought to establish myself as a bona fide College Hippie Mama. The freshman fifteen that had melted away due to the mandatory calisthenics sessions required of every sophomore acting major came back with a vengeance, following skinny Randall's discovery that a handful or two of shredded cheddar enhanced my meatless entrées immeasurably. Pumpkin stew, sweet-potato croquettes,

Custard-Topped Turnip and Bulgur Bake, Carrots à la Grecque, Mushroom 'n' Onion Mockloaf . . . I swear, it took so long to chop all those root vegetables, I had to register pass/fail for Highlights of Astronomy and drop karate altogether. The recipes I was drawn to simmered for a minimum of two hours, giving me plenty of time to reconfigure the refrigerator to accommodate the gallon or so of leftovers that would molder there indefinitely, or at least until Randall and Clyde got together to demand that I deal with them. Even when fresh from the pot, this hearty peasant fare was lumpy, sludge-colored, and certain to produce a lot of flatulence.

"You're so nurturing," Mr. Swain complimented, manfully choking down a brick-sized serving of Vegetarian Shepherd's Pie as I padded around barefoot in a floor-length skirt sewed from an Indian bedspread, an Oscar the Grouch–ish sweater from Amvets, and the souvenir apron from *Sweeney Todd* my mother had purchased in a store devoted entirely to swag from Broadway musicals. "Um, do you have any salt? Or any other kind of seasoning?"

While my entrées were tumbling down the rabbit hole of vegetarianism, my desserts never wandered far from my bourgeois roots. Those underpants-print ramekins got quite a workout as I whipped up batch after batch of *pots de crème*, using a recipe that called for twelve ounces of best-quality chocolate, a pint of heavy cream, and someone with a fake ID convincing enough to secure a bottle of Cointreau from the liquor store next to the Oak Street Market. (Failing that, there was a sinister operation just outside the city limits that made a fortune delivering booze to Northwestern students, no questions asked. Back when I lived in the dorm, the driver used to announce his arrival by calling up on the in-house phone and whispering, "It's cocktail hour.") The flourless chocolate cake I baked from Martha Stewart's *Entertaining* for Lisa Hickey's twenty-first birthday party absorbed a full twenty-four hours, more if the stopwatch started ticking from the moment the raisins were set to soak in a mixing bowl of Jack Daniels.

In a production only slightly less ambitious than heart-shaped waffles, I cranked out mass quantities of brownies, wreath-shaped cornflake cookies, and homemade ladyfingers for a combination dessert and Christmas-caroling party to which the entire acting class had been invited. To keep things from seeming too Betty Crocker, hot buttered rum was served in such quantities that when we singers staggered in from caroling, freezing and mildly buzzed, we found Sarah Cohen, Abra Weissman, Randall, and Peggy O'Brian (whose excuse was sensitivity to extreme cold) lurching around with the tablecloth, re-creating the "I Feel Pretty" number from *West Side Story*.

Yes, given the fresh fruit compotes and baked apples I'd seen masquerading as dessert in the vegetarian cookbooks, I was more than happy to step outside the hippie guise at meal's end. It was only temporary, of course. Picking up where I'd left off was as easy as lighting a stick of incense or pickling a bushel of cucumbers in my Amvets Mason jars.

*

My culinary efforts netted much more positive feedback than anything I managed to do in service of my major. The most vocal of my admirers were single male acquaintances, who'd come by to drop off some sheet music for Clyde or to rehearse a fairy scene from *A Midsummer Night's Dream* but wound up staying to dinner on my invitation. It wasn't sexual—I had Mr. Swain—but I can't say I didn't get off on all that lavish praise. One new friend seemed to regard me as a supernatural being on par with the Mighty Isis, just because he'd caught me wielding a bottle of raspberry vinegar. Another couldn't get over the fact that the bulk raw oats he'd noticed me transferring to a rinsed-out mayonnaise jar were not an acting class prop, but rather something I actually planned upon eating.

"You're amazing," a mild, prematurely balding fellow from Randall's stage-combat club marveled, accepting a second helping of thrice-reheated lentil soup. "Do you cook like this all the time?" Poor guy, he must have been subsisting on nothing but peanut butter sandwiches and generic macaroni and cheese.

I needed all the affirmation I could get because the prolonged falling-out with Clyde did a number on me. I was a bit flip earlier when I said we threw him out because of his Carol Channing imitations. In reality, that was just part of it. After a lot of screaming and shouting, punctuated with stagy expressions of concern for the other's mental well-being, he up and disappeared for several days. I felt certain that he had thrown himself into icy Lake Michigan, especially after Abra Weissman told me she'd never forgive me if anything had happened to him.

This made me terribly uneasy. She was someone I regarded as a person of high moral character, an impression made manifold when I slept with her boyfriend sophomore year. It pained me that someone so ethically above reproach was on record as holding me at least partially accountable should Clyde snuff himself. Fortunately, he hadn't. Randall finally tracked him to the couch of an imperious, allegedly brilliant misfit who'd recently returned from a semester abroad. When he at last deigned to come home, I forgot the numerous pledges I'd made to kick his ass if he turned up alive, sobbing, "We were so worried about you!"

"I find that hard to believe . . . honey!" he snapped. *Whoa.* He sounded less like his old Carol Channing self than some bitchy, middle-aged queen making fun of Bette Davis, circa *All About Eve.* I felt flensed. How could it be that I, the Indian bedspread–wearing, bran muffin–baking Übernurturer wasn't camp enough for the new Clyde? He wasn't really coming back. He just couldn't stand being separated from his Barbra Streisand records while he searched for a new living situation. After that stinging rejoinder in which he'd reduced me to "honey," he disappeared into his room and remained embedded there for three agonizing weeks. It was sort of like having mice. We never saw him, just the evidence that pointed to his existence. Once, he left a knife, smeary with peanut butter, in the middle of the kitchen counter. Another morning, we awoke to find a puddle of ramen noodles sloshed all over the stove.

"Fuck you, Clyde!" Randall shouted at the ceiling. "Just because we can't continue living together doesn't mean you're free to turn the whole apartment into a sty like your disgusting room! I know you hear me!"

In response, Clyde cranked the volume on a sickeningly upbeat Bette Midler song he had taken to broadcasting in a passive-aggressive fury. The Divine Ms. M had squeezed the word "friends" into the refrain more times than I could bear to count.

"This is terrible," I moaned, standing at the counter, half-heartedly poking at the Wheaties Randall had poured for us from a box upon which CLYDE was scrawled in thick black caps. "I can't stand knowing he's up there, listening, waiting for us to leave so he can come down."

"It's not your fault he gets to lie in the bed he made himself," Randall countered from the dining room table. "Leaving dirty peanut butter knives all over the place. He did that to spite us, you know."

"Maybe it's a cry for help."

"Would you please quit being such a doormat?" Randall snorted. "Stop worrying about his feelings. Believe me, he doesn't care about yours. You should hear what he's been saying about you!"

"What's he saying about me?"

"Oh, you know, it's not anything, really. He's just running around the theater building, telling anyone who'll listen that you put on a big act like you're so sweet and nurturing, always making stuff to eat and listening to Joni Mitchell and giving backrubs and, you know, all that Lisa Hickey hippie shit, when in reality you're this total backstabbing bitch who betrays her friends and—" I sank to the unmopped floor with a wail. "Oh, for god's sake, it's nothing to cry about! Ayun. Ayun, you're being ridiculous."

"Who told you? How do you know that's what he's saying?"

"Abra told me," he said, a certain crispness creeping into his tone, "in confidence. Apparently she and Clyde had some big heart-to-heart. Do you mind if I use the rest of the milk? I want another bowl." Seized by involuntary, hiccuping breaths at the authority this lent to Clyde's assessment of my character, I could but gesture blindly toward the fridge.

"Is that a yes?" He stepped over my body, then paused before the open refrigerator, which was packed to capacity with unidentifiable tinfoil wads, a botched sourdough starter I still harbored delusions of making right, and multiple tubs of miso corn chowder that had exceeded its shelf life before Clyde disappeared.

"Oh, look at that. That little Melissa girl who turned up murdered last week is still on the back of our milk carton." He sniffed the spout. "You think it's okay to drink?" No reply. "I don't want to get diarrhea!" he cried, goggling his eyes and making pooping noises in an unsuccessful bid to cheer me up.

The sprightly opening bars of *Friends* cascaded down the stairs for the eighth time that morning. Randall glared at the ceiling, then returned his attention to me.

"Pull yourself together. He'll be out of here before long, and then we'll throw a big fondue party to celebrate. What's the matter? Don't you like fondue? No? Not even chocolate fondue?"

Poor Randall. Nothing sucks worse than trying to coax a laugh from a tough house.

"How 'bout a big ol' heaping helping of diarrhea fondue?"

I assumed the fetal position. "All right, have it your way, but at least eat your Wheaties."

Finally, Clyde moved out and his room was sublet to a meek graduate student who left every Friday afternoon to spend the weekend with her boyfriend downstate. Randall had been serious about throwing a party as a way of closing the door on the Clyde era, but the last time we'd hosted a big bash, some kids from the neighborhood had stolen the tap right out of our backyard while we were groggily groping toward breakfast. Besides, we couldn't very well ask our new housemate to chip in for her third of the keg when she'd be spending the entire clambake in Carbondale. "It's not that I'm opposed to big parties," I told Randall. "I just feel like right now what I need more than anything is to surround myself with supportive, nonjudgmental people."

"We can . . . do that . . . I suppose," he said, looking dubious. "Were you thinking of a, uh, dinner party?" (I could tell he was thinking about the time I showed him my *Alice's Restaurant Cookbook,* the part where the author asserts that unexpected guests can eat off of rinsed hubcaps, should their number exceed the available plates.)

"Well, actually, the weather's getting so nice, I was thinking it would be pleasant to have a little barbeque. I mean, we've got that hibachi that came with the house. We might as well use it."

Randall crossed his arms. "Forgive me if I'm being obtuse here, but aren't you a big vegetable-head these days?"

"I have a recipe for lentil burgers."

"You're joking."

"Come on, they're just like hamburgers except they don't have meat in them. I'll get buns, mustard, ketchup . . . please?" It took some convincing, but finally, Randall gave his consent. In addition to Mr. Swain and Lisa Hickey, I invited an earthy-crunchy senior whose legs were even hairier than mine, her angelic-faced roommate, and an uncommonly modest friend of Randall's who'd turned down a role on a sitcom because he thought the show perpetuated racist stereotypes. I didn't know them very well, but they were the only people I could think of who wouldn't make fun of the menu.

I bought the same brand of charcoal my father had always used to grill steaks. The picture on the bag was enough to make me nostalgic for those summer evenings when I used to squat beside my childhood hibachi, intentionally downwind of the smoke, licking Lawry's Seasoned Salt off my palm. I'd entertained the possibility of spiking the lentil burgers with Lawry's, but then thought better of it, in case retribution turned out to be the reward for deviation. I was already a bit spooked that the recipe seemed near identical to the one for lentil soup.

"Maybe they sort of firm up if you let them sit for a while," Mr. Swain remarked as the patties I was trying to form dripped uncooperatively through my fingers. His optimism was gallant, especially since he was a frequent visitor to Evanston's only fast-food joint, a twenty-four-hour Burger King the students had nicknamed the BK Lounge. "Maybe if you put them in the freezer for a while. Or what about adding some milk or some pancake mix or something?"

Shut up, shut up, shut up, I thought. I knew that he meant well, but really, at this critical juncture, his blind suggestions were the opposite of helpful. Possibly the new housemate, just two credits shy of a master's in chemical engineering, could have come up with a game plan for remedying the looseness of my burgers, but she was in Carbondale with Don or Ron or whatever her boyfriend's name was. Lon.

"Ooh, I didn't know we were getting soup, too," Randall said, glancing over my shoulder as he swanned in from god knows where with a bag full of fencing foils.

"Not soup," Mr. Swain corrected with the nonnegotiable calm of a sapper dismantling a particularly tricky land mine. "Burgers. And I'm sure they'll taste delicious."

Maybe they would have, if they hadn't slithered off the grill onto the hot coals the moment they were tipped out of the slotted spoon bought for a recipe requiring poached eggs. "Look at 'em go," whooped the guests, who had consumed nearly three-quarters of a box of white zinfandel while waiting in vain for the uncooked "patties" to achieve something resembling solidity.

"Oh my god, that is too funny," Randall gasped as he lurched off to pee in a corner of the yard.

"I'll have another one of those buns," the boy who'd rejected the sitcom volunteered. "They're really good!"

"They really are," agreed the angel-faced roommate, reaching into the bag. "Did you get them at Oak Street?"

"Wait, try this," Hairy Legs said, scraping a few pathetic

remnants off the grill with my Amvets spatula. "Get a couple of tomato slices and then sprinkle these over like bacon bits!"

"Oh my god!"

"You're a genius!"

"It's too bad Hickey couldn't make it. She's really missing out."

Mr. Swain slipped his arm around my shoulders, his relief palpable. Things couldn't have worked out any better if I'd planned it. In fact, had the burgers held their shape, it seems likely that the evening would have lost much of its luster. Something alchemical was in the air, impossible to re-create, even if we'd tried. The six of us never came together again, and if we had, I can't imagine that lentil burgers would have been on the menu.

"You don't have any marshmallows, do you?" Hairy Legs asked, still poking at the coals with the spatula.

I shook my head apologetically.

"Wait! Ayun! Think!" Randall pitched a bun at my head and grinned expectantly. "Top shelf, behind the wheat germ and that nasty women's tea. Clyde's Jet-Puffs. From the caroling party, remember? When he insisted we should have cocoa in case somebody didn't drink?"

"He didn't take them? He took everything else."

"Please! He left them to spite us! He never resealed the bag. They're hard as rocks." I opened my mouth to protest, but Randall cut me off. "I know you've got mousse, but really, I can't think of anything more perfect to go with your lentil burgers. It's—what's that word you always use? Serendipity." He flashed me the peace sign as our guests set about partially denuding the forsythia bush belonging to the econ majors next door, ensuring that we'd have more than enough toasting sticks to go around.

veggie burgers

You know you're on the right track when there's roasted, salted peanuts and not a lentil in sight.

Steam 5 oz of spinach, squeeze the moisture out (that bamboo sushi rolling mat you never use might come in handy here), and chop coarsely.

Grate 1 cup of carrots and ½ cup of turnip. If you don't like turnips, go tell it to some other root vegetable.

Slice a scallion nice and thin. Keep slicing until you've got 2 tablespoons.

Mix those veggies together with:

1 teaspoon of salt
2 tablespoons of soy sauce
2 teaspoons of sugar
⅓ cup of chopped dry-roasted peanuts (hooray!)

Beat 2 eggs and add them to the veggies.

Use that rolling mat to squeeze the moisture out of a 14-oz block of tofu, then mash it even more with a fork, then put it out of its misery by putting it into the veggies.

Turn on some Arlo Guthrie, take off your diamond rings, and attempt to shape this mess into little patties of about ⅓ cup each. It's sloppy, but they should hold together fairly well. If your bottom lip is quivering, add a tablespoon or two of semolina, or even some bulk-bin cornmeal.

Fry both sides of the patties in hot oil until they turn golden brown. If the hibachi starts whispering seductively, shout, "Get behind me, Satan!" in a voice loud enough to wake the econ majors next door.

Serve on toasted buns with all the trimmings you'd expect on a "real" burger. Advanced students might want to try some wasabi mayonnaise.

wasabi mayonnaise

Mix some wasabi with some mayonnaise.

Really, everything tastes better when mixed with mayonnaise.

postcoital breakfast

It's been quite a while since I've had a true postcoital breakfast. Oh, I have sex and then eventually granola, but it's not the same. I blame the children, of course, but also the dearth of dirty diners in this neighborhood. No doubt I'm romanticizing my sordid youth, but I seem to recall that once upon a time, under the right circumstances, dusty decor and unwashed aprons were hallmarks of unparalleled deliciousness. Our corner diner, popular with both Department of Corrections staffers and employees of the bail-bond joints nearby, looks plenty gross, but the food has never delivered on the promise of its dingy stuffed sailfish and dark, faux-wood paneling.

Maybe I'd feel differently if Greg and I had just met and there were no children crawling in bed with us at the crack of dawn. Jesus, these days, the idea of sneaking around the corner with the Sunday *Times* qualifies as an erotic fantasy, if only because there's so little chance of its becoming reality. What with all the fur-lined handcuffs and whipped cream licking and pedicured toe sucking and *harder harder oh yes fuck me harder* going on in the movies, I feel kind of ripped off that the money shot is invariably withheld. When are we going to see Nicole Kidman and Jude Law lollygagging in a ripped vinyl booth, using their toast to mop up the leftover yolk from their ravaged plates? There are some things Hollywood never gets right.

Actually, even I have trouble picturing any of today's reigning romantic leads in Rocky's Luncheonette, a dive my happy memories have covered in something like barnacles. Lookswise, it was better suited to horror, or maybe an indie thriller, one of those scenes where a pair of thuggish would-be assassins get their marching orders from the preternaturally quiet boss who will later torture them to death for botching the job.

Situated in a small storefront on a particularly downtrodden commercial strip of Chicago's far north side, Rocky's was a five-minute walk from the two studio apartments where I was getting to know Isaac, my coworker and neighbor, a whole lot better. Sandwiched between a liquor store where crack pipes outsold Rolling Rock and a ghostly apothecary that displayed jars of colored water alongside toilets for invalids, it was practically invisible, its plate glass window opaque from years of accumulated grime.

Given that the Heartland Café, a celebrated hippie-style eatery with outdoor seating, all-day tofu scrambles, and chili-pepper lights galore, was even closer to where we lived, it seems odd that Isaac and I would ever have wandered across Rocky's threshold. But once we did, we were hooked, suddenly regulars whose idiosyncrasies were a matter of public record: He required his water without ice. I would go through an entire monkey dish of creamers every time my coffee was refilled. The only kind of jelly he could deal with was mixed fruit.

Our courtship was still new enough that buying a newspaper in order to ignore each other for separate sections was still a form of foreplay, but in the eyes of Mrs. Rocky we were an established couple, the skinny boy who did the crossword puzzle and the girl who propped her feet in his lap. I loved it that our union, still the cause of gossip and innuendo at the restaurant where we worked, was here taken for granted, sustained by regular orders, a usual booth, and no secondary characters, save the benign Mrs. Rocky, who knew only that we were young, we were in love, and we out-tipped the bulk of her reprobate clientele.

Mrs. Rocky purchased the luncheonette from Rocky, its original owner, then resisted all temptation to fix the joint up in any way. Okay, she did type a few dishes from her native Korea onto the bottom of the dog-eared menus, beneath preexisting listings for silver-dollar pancakes and corned beef hash. Scuffing between the refrigerator and the grill in well-worn Dearfoams, she was equally conversant in hash browns and *chap chae*, if not much English.

"It's like being a kid, when you spend the night at a friend's house and the next day, his mom gets up and cooks breakfast for you," Isaac observed as Mrs. Rocky poured orange juice into scratched plastic glasses. Yes, except I couldn't come up with a single childhood pal whose mother's kitchen featured a stuffed pheasant, sticky from untold years of improper ventilation and zero dusting. Also, both the physical explorations and Oriental food of my youth were way, way tamer than the stuff in which I currently indulged, in the booth at Rocky's and a couple of neighboring boudoirs. Then it was all canned water chestnuts and some light stroking with clipped fingernails, not that anyone's mother would have served water chestnuts, or even mandarin oranges in heavy syrup, for breakfast.

*

Perhaps because I spent the first decade of my life in horror of bacon and eggs, I've never been someone who insists on traditional American breakfast food for breakfast. Having greeted the day with everything from cold pizza to a couple of handfuls of Halloween candy, I have to say that Mrs. Rocky's *bi bim bop* was something special, perhaps because it was my first, and also, I was exerting myself in all sorts of appetite-increasing ways. Steamed spinach, shredded carrots, bean sprouts, and scraps of *bulgolgi* covered a huge mound of rice served in something akin to a metal dog-food dish. A sizable dollop of homemade chili paste lurked to one side. A fried egg glistened atop, waiting to be bashed apart so its yolk could glaze the whole. At the end of the feed, when no food remained in my bowl, I would suck my chopsticks, feeling equally nostalgic for those little paddle-shaped disposable wooden ice cream spoons and the meal I had just eaten.

"This place is so amazing," I'd sigh, stretching lazily, luxuriating in that sated-but-not-stuffed feeling that drives mankind to cap high-impact carnal aerobics with a wholesome hot breakfast, whenever possible. "I swear I'd die happy if we never went anywhere else."

I suppose I should note that with one exception, nobody of our acquaintance got the appeal of Rocky's. That's not from lack of trying on our part. We were as eager as newlyweds to let others bask in this aspect of our love. First his mother, then mine, were taken to be introduced to Mrs. Rocky, who blushed and apologized for her English and shifted from foot to foot in her dingy Dearfoams as the mothers not so surreptitiously polished their forks with paper napkins. When I dragged my college friends down, one squint through the window was enough to convince them we'd be better off braving the Heartland's waitlist.

No one but Isaac's gentle, misanthropic best friend Arthur could appreciate that Rocky's was a diamond in the rough. Actually, Arthur's girlfriend, Drake-Ann, liked it too, braying at the pheasant and accidentally knocking the syrup over whilst waving her cigarette, but then, Drake-Ann was a restaurant person, too. The four of us worked together, in fact. Or we did until Drake-Ann and Isaac were discovered to be cuckolding Arthur and me with each other, which, standard restaurant melodrama though it may have been, still stung. Their deal-breaking dalliance also brought my Rocky's idyll to a screeching halt. I sniffled my way through one final meal there, seated across from Arthur, who chain-smoked Marlboros and needlessly mutilated the jellies, stolidly insisting that he'd moved on. I wonder what Mrs. Rocky made of us, coming in without Isaac like that.

Shortly thereafter I moved out of the neighborhood, and the next time I found myself on that block, Rocky's was gone, replaced by some truly featureless operation, some clinic or a plumbing parts store, I forget. Its demise seemed a fitting tribute to Isaac's and my broken love, though a shame because Isaac's successor, Wylie, would have dug it to pieces. That one had a real taste for dirty.

So many postcoital breakfast spots gone! Ruby's, where the octogenarian proprietress would sometimes take a break to run her hand through Issac's predecessor Nate's lank blond locks, then return to the grill without so much as rinsing her gnarled hands. To the best of my knowledge, Ruby's was the only place on the north side of Chicago where one could get grits without irony or salt pork, period.

Before Ruby's, and Nate, there was the Sherman Snack Shop, a Greek diner where I, like many Northwestern coeds, used whichever hand wasn't currently entwined in that of the latest flame to paw at chocolate chip pancakes oozing butter and Reddi-wip. The possibility of bumping into at least a dozen people we knew only added to the illicit thrill of the lushly abundant calories, the paid-for-but-skipped breakfast back at the dorm, the assigned chapters scotched in favor of something Starland Vocal Band would call "afternoon delight."

Having spent the summer between junior and senior year waitressing at Sherm's, benevolently bestowing postcoital breakfasts (PCBs) on languorous, smiling deuces with dark circles under their eyes, I can attest that despite its bright corner location and orange vinyl upholstery, the place was a roach pit. They congregated near the industrial-sized refill jugs of maple syrup, some long dead, others weakly waving what limbs they could, trapped by ancient, unwiped spills. Nearly as scary was the dishwashing room, where Otis, an alcoholic, meth-addicted Screamin' Jay Hawkins lookalike, somehow managed to maintain inch-and-a-half-long fingernails caked with dirt. Not that having the inside scoop on my employer's hygienic shortcomings could deter me from coming in with Mr. Swain on romantic mornings off. Come on, where else were we going to go? J. K. Sweets? The Hut? That brass-railed fern bar with the Dixieland brunch? The Sherman Snack Shop was the place for collegiate PCBs. Rounding Sherm's corner late one morning shortly after we'd broken up, it about killed me to glimpse Mr. Swain through the window, tenderly offering a forkful of his Combination Special to my replacement.

I'm sure the cleanliness standards of Walker Bros., the stained-glass and polished-wood pancake house a short drive up Green Bay Road from Northwestern, were such that the frostily well-to-do homemaker Mary Tyler Moore played in *Ordinary People* would have approved. No doubt it still enjoys cultish devotion among Northwestern parents who make the trip to see how their tuition checks are being spent. Over the course of my college career, I managed to consume several skillet-sized apple pancakes there, as well as a lifetime supply of lingonberries, always in the company of my rapturous mother or equally bedazzled grandparents. Never with someone whose belt buckle I was just dying to undo . . . unless we're counting the time my grandmother wanted to meet Mr. Swain, a libido dampener if ever there was.

I know Greg and I wallowed through our share of postcoital breakfasts in the springtime of our union, when his reputation was still that of a ladykiller and mine a serial monogamist. Unfortunately, it appears that moths have spent the last decade and a half feasting on my memories of our first couple hundred breakfasts. Where did we go?

Before we moved in together, he, his two forks, one plate, and more paper carryout napkins than I could count lived in a mildewed studio apartment near the Melrose Diner, a twenty-four-hour hot spot I disliked out of loyalty to a waitress friend who'd been fired when the register's drawer didn't synch up with the nightly total. I have a vague recollection of sitting across from Greg whilst peeling one of those bananas that garnished every Melrose entrée, but our friend Phil was there, too, which means it couldn't have been a true postcoital breakfast. Forensically, I'm inclined to pinpoint this meeting around two in the morning, since the only time I could stomach the Melrose was when I found myself sporting a serious french fry johnson after every diner that hadn't fired a friend of mine had shuttered up for the night.

So where the hell did Greg and I go, if not the Melrose? Ann Sather? Nookies? Nookies Too? I guess I could venture out onto a limb and say Manny's, though I'm hesitant since that was the site of many well-remembered PCBs with Greg's immediate predecessor, Wylie. On the other hand, Manny's Belgian waffles were such that it would have been a crying shame to throw the baby out with the bathwater. Sanitarily speaking, the bustling, brightly lit Manny's was in an entirely different league than my previous PCB spots. The matronly waitresses were tidy souls from the tips of their beehives to the toes of their polished nurse shoes, and the busboys proved efficient and cheery wipers. Any hairs in the eggs were certain to have come from my rumpled head. Perhaps such cleanliness was a fitting shift, given that I was sharing syrup with the man I would eventually marry, if indeed we ever actually went to Manny's in each other's postcoital company. It stands to reason that we would have, since it served breakfast all day and was located just half a block from my apartment. Still, it's a bit unnerving that every time I try to place myself across from Greg in one of Manny's red booths, the face that's peeking over the top of his menu belongs to Wylie.

The evolution of our relationship explains why Greg is the only "boyfriend" whose breakfasts have been allowed to fade. It's not unlike the phenomenon I experience when trying to remember my eight-year-old daughter in her infancy.

Intellectually, I accept that eight years ago, there was this baby to whom I was inextricably linked. Sleepless nights, blown-out diapers, and several little outfits return in vivid detail, but it's nigh impossible to reconcile myself to the idea that that baby was long-haired, long-limbed Inky, the budding recorder-player littering our small apartment with her size-13 shoes and half-finished fan mail to the boy who played Peter in *The Chronicles of Narnia.* This is the baby I so brazenly suckled, often for hours at a time?

Greg and I have accrued so many layers since joining forces, we'd need professional mining equipment to drill all the way down to pancakes as something akin to a physical-contact marathon's Gatorade station. Down around the igneous layer are our brunch dates with other childless adults, all the times we met Karen and her first husband, Chet, for *huevos rancheros* at Angel's. Or lingered over endless refills of coffee with Phil and whomever he happened to be dating at that sunny joint that was closer to his place than to ours, the one with the vintage Coca-Cola signs and those little wooden bar games you play with golf tees. Somewhere among the arrowheads lay our former travels, from Southeast Asia's fresh-fruit salads and ubiquitous banana pancakes to the time Greg was served a glass of fresh-squeezed orange Fanta in a Romanian hotel. Deposited among the sedimentary layer, we discover first Inky, then Milo, both of them prepared to put up a squall should the parent on the short end of the staying-in-bed-on-a-Saturday stick forget to add chocolate chips to the homemade pancakes they should be thankful to get at all. What do they think I am, a short-order cook? Someone with endless time and energy to devote to their every whim and desire? I'm their mother, not their love-ah! If the little nippers start lobbying for a second batch, I send them Greg's way.

"Go wake your father up and tell him to make you an Egyptian Bull's-Eye." Wow, that sounds like a hell of a euphemism. For what, I'm not entirely sure, but I hope to find out, as soon as we get a bedroom with a door and the kids are old enough to craft their morning meals unattended. An Egyptian Bull's-Eye. I can't speak for my husband, but I'm not sure Mama could manage something of that magnitude without the promise of a big, greasy breakfast afterward.

postcoital pancakes

If I were you, I'd go to a diner.

Failing that, beat an egg in a big mixing bowl.

Add ½ cup of yogurt, ½ cup of milk, and ½ teaspoon of vanilla.

Melt 2 tablespoons of butter and add that.

Pull out the Bromwell's Measuring-Sifter (Pat. No 1,753,995) that you bought in college, put it onto a salad plate, and pour in:

½ cup of white flour

½ cup of wheat flour (maybe mixed with some almond meal)

¾ teaspoon of salt

2 tablespoons of sugar

1 teaspoon of baking powder

¼ teaspoon of baking soda (and you know what? One time I got powder confused with soda and the pancakes turned out just fine, if a bit on the seltzery side.)

Hold the sifter over the mixing bowl, remove the salad plate, and let it rip! Stir the wet into the dry. Get your mind out of the gutter.

If you have children, they will probably expect you to add M&Ms at this point, but maybe they spent the night at a friend's house, in which case, you should definitely go to a diner. If that's not in the cards this morning, drop onto a hot, lightly oiled griddle (the batter, not the children).

pad thai mi mai

If I were to cite just one lesson gleaned from years of bumming around Southeast Asia, it'd be a toss-up between "Beware the Australian Pizza" and "If the Monkey Take Your Camera, Let the Monkey Have Your Camera." Fortunately, I never met a monkey who exhibited anything more than blasé lack of interest in my beat-up, secondhand Nikon. Still, it seemed like good advice to have on a sign in Bali's famous Monkey Forest, as well as a maxim worthy of inclusion in one's governing principles. Not a day goes by that I don't try to let the monkey have my camera, at least metaphorically.

The Australian Pizza is an entirely different matter, possibly because I had a direct run-in with it. Isaac and I were seasoned travelers by the time I ordered it in an otherwise deserted open-air restaurant overlooking an Indonesian surfers' beach that heavy fog had wiped clean of surfers. "Are you sure you don't want *gado-gado* or something?" Isaac asked when told of my choice, a good twenty minutes or so before the establishment's scion shuffled over, order pad in hand.

"I am sick unto death of *gado-gado*," I replied peevishly. Leaving our friends had put an unexpected strain on this relationship. We'd been a cute enough couple on American soil, but we were failing miserably at the trip-long assignment of being everything else to each other, too. Given that it had been more than a decade since my menu choices had been subject to parental approval, his attempt to dissuade me from the only thing that sounded good did not sit well. "And don't tell me to get *nasi goreng.* I hate *nasi goreng!*"

"What about *nasi campur?*" he suggested, scanning the menu, a handwritten, poorly laminated single-sheeter.

"I don't want *nasi* anything!" I snapped. "What I want is a vacation from Indonesian food!"

"Yeah, but Australian pizza?" he countered, looking down the long nose I had, in less stressful times, considered pretty as a pony's.

"Jesus, they just call it that because Australia's like, what, four hundred miles away or something? If we were in Mexico, it'd probably be called 'American pizza.' Look at the ingredients! 'Tomatoe saus and cheez.'"

"I just think it's smarter to stick with what the locals eat, since that's what they know how to cook."

"Yes, I know, we read the same section in the guidebook. I have been eating what the locals eat for the last five months. In fact, I seem to recall sticking with fish-ball soup when someone else was going to throw a tantrum if he didn't get to go to that Burger King in Jakarta, so if you don't mind, I think I'll go ahead and order what I want to order, just this once."

"Okaaay," he exhaled, his tone conveying that I was (a) making a big mistake and (b) a total bitch. Turns out he was right on both counts, though sluggish service delayed confirmation for at least an hour and a half. Mad as I was, I struggled mightily to fill that interval with conversation, terrified that we could be seen as one of those sad-sack couples with nothing to say to each other in restaurants. Not that there was anyone to see us but the waiter, who'd been AWOL so long, I worried that he had gone home.

"Maybe he's killing the chicken for your *satay*," I whispered with forced jollity. Isaac shrugged and gazed out at the fog. Hardly a sidesplitter to begin with, the threadbare joke lacked whatever comic incongruity it might have had in our country of origin. There, the journey to the table commenced in a walk-in freezer. Here, any animal smaller than a fire hydrant was probably hanging around the kitchen in a basket, waiting for its death sentence to be carried out on the premises.

"No, I'll bet he's out picking peanuts for your peanut sauce," I revised, though Isaac's posture made clear that he was no longer even pretending to listen to my prattle. Or maybe he was listening but was pretending not to, to demonstrate his loathing for me. We seemed to have hit a new low, but things were bound to improve as soon as my pizza arrived. How could they not? Nothing like a little comfort food from home to remedy a relationship sorely taxed by so much time spent joined at the hip, fighting about maps, money, and now, apparently, what I should or shouldn't order in restaurants. It was insane. The pizza would make it all better, though. Pizza was an integral part of our romantic history. We had fallen in love working in a restaurant that served wonderfully unfussy thin-crusts molten with mozzarella and other goodies. Ooh, what I wouldn't have given for one of Dave's spinach-and-garlics right then, maybe half-sausage, the way Isaac liked.

"Isaac, you can share my pizza," I offered in lieu of an apology. "If it ever gets here."

No sunset was visible through that dense fog, but I imagine

the sun must have been slinking toward the horizon by the time the waiter finally reemerged. In one hand, he carried a platter of *satay*; in the other, a pancake thickly spread with ketchup, and half a raw onion bulging dead center, like a yolk.

G'day, mate! Thit's how we like 'em Down Under!

While I stared down in disbelief, Isaac silently extended a stick of *satay*, as if proffering his condolences. I was so traumatized that I didn't pick another fight for at least four hours.

The first time I left American soil to go gadding about Europe, my boyfriend Nate and I took just $800 to cover six weeks' worth of accommodation, food, and entertainment. Not surprisingly, we often wound up dining on bread in the train stations where we slept. The vagabonding lifestyle agreed with me, but I quickly realized that next time, I'd do better to travel in warm climates where I could afford to eat. And ever since that first bite of spanakopita, I'd had a hankering for foods not widely available in the American Midwest.

That's not entirely accurate. From a culinary standpoint, the world I set out to explore in the early 1990s was already much smaller than the one in which I'd grown up. By the time I graduated from college, a city dweller like me didn't have to leave the country to gobble all-you-can-eat buffets of *saag paneer, aloo gobi,* and butter *naan*, bask in lemongrass-scented steam from a Mongolian hot pot, or scoop up *sik sik wat* with an edible baldskin wig the menu cryptically referred to as "Ethiopian Bread." Hell, the adventurous palate could get all that and more at Taste of Chicago, a weeklong alfresco food festival that annually turned

Grant Park into an Antietam of picked-over frog legs and buffalo wings. As happy as I was to find the world at my doorstep every summer, I resented the disproportionate expense of the Taste's Dixie Cup–sized portions, as well as its interminable lines.

I learned soon enough that Taste of Chicago's queues were strictly bush league compared to India's, but five cents for a cup of *masala chai* in its country of origin seemed a more than reasonable tradeoff. Something that delicious would've run me at least three tickets at Taste of Chicago, after which I'd have had to fight my way to an unoccupied spot on the trashy lawn. My precious Styrofoam cup would have been jostled all to hell by the enormous Lycra-sheathed heiners of fellow festivalgoers who drove in from other midwestern states, only to put themselves on a strict diet of deep-dish, Chicago-style pizza, french fries, and massive quantities of Bud Light. "I ain't eatin' none of that weird shit," was such a commonly overheard utterance, I liked to think of it as the Taste's unofficial slogan.

You'd think a formerly picky eater might show some sympathy for the buzz-cut lunks whose beer-addled girlfriends kept harping after them to try courtesy bites of such bunny slopes as tamales and jerk chicken, but by this point, my heart was firmly with the rebellion. Once I started pursuing my travel bug in earnest, a "taste of" anything was not going to be enough. As toothsome as the exotic, doll-sized portions it doled out may have been, no temporary structure of yellow vinyl lashed to metal piping could supply the context I craved. I wanted my chai in a diminutive, unglazed clay cup I could throw out the window when I was finished, same as any other passenger on the slow train to Calcutta. And while I was at it, might as well plunk down a few rupees more for some *channa masala*, an oily snack of dried chickpeas, curried chow-mein noodle thingies, and assorted twiglike bits I was hard pressed to identify. Delicious! It always bugged me that in all of the time we spent together on Indian trains, I could never persuade Greg to try more than a nibble. "I'm telling you, it's completely addictive," I'd tell him, pushing a rolled newspaper coneful under his nose. "It's the Chex Mix of India!"

"No thank you."

"But it's so good!" I woofed, plunging a paw heavy with recently purchased rings into the depths of the cone.

"I can see that you think so," he agreed, glancing meaningfully at my shirtfront.

"Try some," I squawked, unconcerned as a few tidbits scattered like birdseed.

"Ayunee," he said sternly, brushing off his paperback copy of *Midnight's Children*. "It's rolled up in a sheet of old newspaper. Did you get a good look at the kid who sold it to you?" I tossed my head impatiently. "Did you notice the condition of his hands?"

"Fine, more for me," I retorted, but Greg had been goaded into one of those moods where he can't rest until his point has been driven home.

"What do you think he does with those hands of his? What does he use for toilet paper?"

"I don't know," I sassed, knowing full well. "Maybe he used newspaper, this very sheet."

"He uses his hands," Greg continued. "The same hands he uses to scoop up that gerbil food you persist in eating, despite knowing the sanitary conditions under which it came to be."

I believe this is what's known as a "Mexican standoff." The frequency with which they occurred sunk Isaac and me before the ink on our passports could dry, but for some odd reason, they continue to lend a certain piquancy to my interactions with Greg.

"You don't know what you're missing," I insisted, when it looked like he was returning to his book.

I can't remember if this was before or after he fell prey to a particularly virulent case of "Delhi Belly," a monthlong ordeal that, by anyone's reckoning, really should have been mine.

Sometimes I look at all the carved masks and traditional tribal instruments clotting up our limited storage space and wonder why we bothered hauling all this shit home when clearly, the best souvenirs are fond recollections of shredded green papaya sprinkled with brown sugar and chili powder, or the crusty, cilantro-spiked *banh mi* of Vietnam. Every time we get *pad thai* from one of the half dozen restaurants who will deliver this dish to our door, I get bittersweet pleasure from thinking of how inferior it is to the magnificent specimen I enjoyed at a card table set up on the side of a road in a dusty town whose name I never knew. *Hijole,* that was good eats.

Who knows how many friends I've bored with the story of the world's best *dal,* dished onto a banana leaf in some anonymous train station where I once made a midnight connection. Personally, I find hearing about foreign foods far more enjoyable than looking at vacation photographs, even my own. In college, my favorite professor was a sweet-tempered cultural anthropologist who held us all rapt with tales from several sabbaticals spent in a Hmong refugee camp on the Mekong River, just across the border from Laos. Once, he told us that the camp elders had offered him first taste from a communal bowl of dried chicken blood seasoned with five-alarm chilies. This he described as a great, if unwanted, honor.

"What did you do?" a pert Tri-Delt in the front row gasped.

"Well, I ate it," Dwight answered with an apologetic smile. "To have refused would have been unspeakably rude." He nodded at the memory, patiently waiting for the screams to die down so he could continue.

Man, I thought as I scribbled the name of the refugee camp in the margins of my notebook. *One of these days, I'm going to take off and have me some adventures like that. Everything except the dried-blood part.*

Eventually, things calmed down enough for Dwight to entertain questions. "Why, yes, Steve!" he cried, twinkling like a woodland elf to see the monolithic football player in the back coming out of his vegetative state in order to raise a tentative paw.

"Uh, okay," Steve hesitated, clearly abashed to be speaking aloud in front of others, "I was just wondering . . . "

"Yes?" Dwight smiled in the encouraging manner of the preternaturally patient.

"Uh," the footballer shifted uncomfortably in a one-armed lecture desk designed for students of more mortal build, "I was wondering if you ever had one of those monkeys where, you know, they screw it into a table and whap the top of its head off, so you can eat the brains right out of the skull?"

You'd be surprised how often that question comes up when people learn you've traveled in Southeast Asia.

*

Having been, I can tell you that monkey brain sashimi served *en corps du* monkey strikes me as more of a special occasion dish than the type of fare locals consume on a day-in-day-out basis. Its complete and conspicuous absence from the street stalls and night markets of my stints in Vietnam, Thailand, Malaysia, Indonesia, and Singapore came as a relief. I'm too squeamish. I got so nervous before my first and only cockfight that I nearly threw up, and I'd eaten plenty of cock in the years leading up to that moment.

Only someone on the prowl for ever-more-bizarre bragging rights screams, "Far out! Reach me that grapefruit spoon!" when confronted with a splatter guard and a screwed-down monkey. It may be exotic, but I refuse to concede that it sounds tasty, in the way a lightly poached hummingbird stuffed with caviar and gold leaf does. If I had to make an educated guess, I'd venture that it tastes like the ammonia drenched adrenal gland of a seriously freaked out monkey, which may taste like chicken for all I know, but does that make it the kind of dish any sane person yearns to savor more than once?

By contrast, the flavors that left me immediately hungry for more are nothing if not humble. Ragged, fried rice cakes spiraled with hardened caramel. Fresh-squeezed orange juice to which sea salt was added with a liberal hand. Wide noodles with pork and broccoli, the only, and therefore signature, dish of an open-to-the-street Banglamphu dive where antique clocks hung atelier-style beside portraits of King Bhumibol. Sweetened condensed milk drizzled over red beans, jackfruit, and chipped ice. Cold chrysanthemum tea packaged in a tiny wax juice box or poured into a plastic bag worn tethered to the wrist with a cleverly attached rubber band. Hell, even green Parrot toilet soap deserves to be rhapsodized. I never ate it, but I did come close to joyful tears when I found it in the Thai Grocery at the mouth of Chicago's Argyle Street. Nothing I've eaten to date, though, can displace mangosteens. Ah, mangosteens. My madeleines, my Lolita.

I'd been in and out of Bangkok on my way to other locales half a dozen times before noticing them, probably because they'd been out of season on my other six trips. Suddenly, though, it was impossible to walk down the street without passing a pyramid of this bizarre fruit. Their appearance was incredibly endearing, if a little hard to describe. Purple leather tennis balls sporting tam o'shanters a size or two too small—how's that? They were so cute, I wanted to throw one against a garage door. "Fruit," the lady who sold me my first dozen answered, when asked what they were called. "This fruit." I was so excited I paid the very first price she quoted me.

"What are you intending to do with those things?" Greg asked, casting a dubious eye at the produce-filled baggie I was swinging around like Lilly's Purple Plastic Purse.

"Eat them, silly! What do you think?"

"Why'd you buy so many?"

"Well, I thought I was buying just one, but I guess the woman I bought them from misunderstood. It's okay. They were only thirty baht."

"Thirty—wait, you were okay with thinking that you were paying more than a dollar for one of those things?"

"How much was the admission to that war museum you went

to the other day?" I challenged, my baggie inscribing a perfect circle just inches from his temple.

"All I'm saying is, I hope you like them."

"Like you like tanks and killing?"

"You will forgive me," he said, chivalrously taking my hand, "if I am incapable of sharing your level of enthusiasm for this sort of thing."

He wasn't just whistling Dixie.

"Oh! Unh! Oh my god, baby!" The walls of the little room we'd taken at the Friendly Guesthouse were thin, but given that we'd probably never see them again, who cared what the neighbors thought? *Slow down, slow down,* I told myself. *Make it last.* I closed my eyes, relishing that ambrosial sensation of satisfaction tangoing with insatiability. The ceiling fan whispered overhead, a discreet if avid witness. Sighing voluptuously, I groped behind me for our well-thumbed copy of *Southeast Asia on a Shoestring.* Toward the front, there was a guide to the region's produce.

Okay, it wasn't *salak,* since those had brown rinds that looked like snakeskin. It couldn't be a custard apple or, alternatively, a *zurzat,* because that fruit's flesh, while white, was also described as "squishy." My tennis balls had the consistency of Hacky Sacks and—bingo!—"cracked open to reveal tasty white segments with a very fine flavor."

"Greg? Greg? Honey, are you awake?"

"Unh."

"I found out what my things are called!"

"Unh."

"Mangosteens. The book says Queen Victoria was offering

this huge reward to anyone who could bring one back to England for her to taste. I can totally see why!"

"Unh."

"Eat some." I seized the nearest mangosteen and rolled it at him.

"I did," he muttered, declining to take this gift, or even open his eyes.

"I swear to god," I chattered happily, retrieving my offering and prying it open with his Swiss Army knife, "this must be what it's like to drink nectar. When I was, like, what, maybe three years old, my grandmother bought me this pack of cards because we were going on a car trip, only not regular cards, it was more like a coloring book, except they were individual cards that came in a pack. Are you following?" Detecting the barest of nods, I plunged on, still quite keen to "share," as Professor Dwight would have called it. "It came with four colored pencils. Anyway, one of the pictures was this beautiful little bumblebee girl perching on a flower like it was a stool. She was sipping from a striped straw jammed into the bell of a bigger flower, a lily if I'm recalling this correctly. I made a total fetish out of that picture. I refused to even color it, I loved it so much. And, this is going to sound crazy—I mean, I haven't thought about that picture in years—but when I peeled that first mangosteen and put a section on my tongue, I swear to god, the first thing that flashed into my mind was that bumblebee girl drinking out of a flower with her straw! I was like, this is what she must have been drinking!"

"Unh."

"Isn't that amazing?"

"I am trying," Greg enunciated, with ominous self-control, "to take a nap. But someone in this room insists on talking." His eyes snapped open as he rolled to face me. "Ho, shit! How many of those things did you eat?" Seven or eight ruined purple husks festooned my side of the bed and looked to be well on their way toward colonizing the floor.

"Relax, I saved you a couple." I jutted my chin at the laminated fiberboard bureau where the fruit lady's plastic bag slumped. "Unless, of course, you don't want them." I raised my eyebrows, hoping I didn't look too much like our friend Heather's terminally peckish boxer, Sydney.

"You're going to get the runs," he predicted pleasantly, flopping back down as he relinquished his stake with a limp wave.

Many times since the frenzied, weeklong mangosteen orgy that followed, I've found myself passionately desiring to reconnect with my bee girl's nectar. If only I'd had such a glorious reaction to lychees or rambutan or even durian, all of which can be found in season in Chinatown and year round at a fashionable Manhattan fruit purveyor whose prices don't seem all that exorbitant when compared to round-trip airfare from JFK to Bangkok. Even if I had that kind of cash to blow, I'm a mother now! I can't go gallivanting halfway across the world just because raspberries and cantaloupe don't really do it for me anymore.

If only I could home in on a domestic source. I've rooted around this city like a pig in search of truffles, but sadly, the closest I've gotten is a fourteen-ounce can of mangosteen sections, packed in heavy syrup. I shelled out but, once home, found I couldn't bring myself to break out the can opener. Not to discount the charm of recognizing that purple tennis ball on the label, but how could the contents possibly compare to those packed in the heavy syrup of nostalgia? The flavor I've internalized is too delicate, too elusive to survive the rigors of a distant cannery.

It mocked me for years, that can, until the November morning I impulsively snatched it from our topmost kitchen shelf and stuck it in Inky's backpack, instructing her to deposit it in the box her school sets out for donations during its annual Thanksgiving food drive. I can only hope that my can found its way to darkest Queens or Brooklyn and into the hands of a needy Thai Gran-Gran who'd be more than psyched to incorporate it into some sort of Siamese Jell-O salad. More likely, it's being used as a doorstop by a recipient who's still stumped for a polite way to let the yuppie do-gooders know that next time, they should err on the side of Success Rice or a Hormel ham. Anything but the dusty exotica they apparently couldn't stomach, either.

monkey brain tartare

No, I'm just shining you on. It's really a recipe for those sandwiches I couldn't get enough of in Vietnam, made with shrimp instead of delicious mystery (monkey?) meat pâté.

Grate a fat carrot. Sprinkle it with 2 tablespoons of seasoned sushi vinegar and then give it some privacy.

Slice half a cucumber movie star thin.

Whittle a couple of scallions into nonuniform lengthwise shards.

Crack open a bag of frozen cooked large shrimp, put them in a bowl, and put the bowl under the tap under a steady trickle of cold water. After 5 minutes, you can pat them dry. Don't forget to pull their tails off, because, to quote Lisa Hickey, you don't want to be crunching through that shit. If you crave warmth or fear bacteria, feel free to squirt them with some citrus and chase them around a frying pan for a minute or two.

Chop a bunch of cilantro (no need to separate out the stems, Dopey) and mix it up with:

- 2½ tablespoons of mayonnaise
- 2½ tablespoons of nonfat yogurt (which will absolve you of any Hellmann's you might have felt the need to sample)
- ¾ teaspoon of fish sauce
- 1 tablespoon of fresh-squeezed lime juice
- either ¼ teaspoon of cayenne or a squirt of hot sauce

Bicycle through traffic clutching a couple of whole-grain baguettes. Saw them in half lengthwise, then cut each baguette into thirds, unless it's just you, pounding down a day's worth of calories, Dagwood style. (If you heated the shrimp, be consistent and heat the baguettes too.)

Slather the baguette bottoms with a generous spoonful of sauce from the earlier paragraph.

Pour the sushi vinegar down the drain, then divide the grated carrot between the baguettes.

Chuck the shrimp in the remaining sauce, toss to coat, and then, in the interest of fairness, eat enough to ensure that no diner will receive more than any other. If you're worried that there won't be enough left to go around, it's time to start dealing them out (possibly after cutting them in half, to make it look like there's more).

Festoon with cucumber and scallions, put the lid on, and eat in the company of those who don't mind if you make a spectacle of yourself. (Serves 6, which, in my book, translates to 3.)

just a sliver

I can pinpoint the exact moment I became a vegetarian. The summer between junior and senior years of high school, I enrolled in a six-week program for stagestruck youth that took place on the campus of the university I would later attend. The "cherubs," as we were called, ate all of our meals in the cafeteria of Allison Hall, the '60s-era dorm in which we were housed. Ever since the acceptance letter had arrived in early March, I'd been bouncing off the walls, giddy to get a taste of the collegiate lifestyle, but many of my fellow cherubs, who hailed from such exotic locations as New York and boarding school, behaved as if our situation was no great shakes.

As I observed from a safe distance, they openly lit up Dunhills, made casual reference to Greenwich Village vintage stores, name-dropped bands I'd never heard of, and slouched around Allison's lobby, criticizing the provincial Midwest. Their exoticism was a birthright they wore lightly. That night, when a hair-netted cafeteria worker manning the entrée station attempted to serve me some roast beef, I demurred, then turned to the kid next to me in line. "I'm a vegetarian," I explained.

"Really?" His awkward posture and faded Florida State T-shirt were reassuring in the midst of so much teenage sophistication. "Why?"

"Oh, animals mostly," I replied with studied nonchalance, nodding when the cafeteria man offered to load me up with garlic bread and canned corn.

"She's a vegetarian," the kid behind me told the kid behind him, a scrawny-looking specimen in rainbow suspenders.

"Really? Don't you ever, like, want to pound down a burger or some McNuggets or something?"

"No," I smiled, as patient and mysterious as anything to emerge from da Vinci's brush.

"Never?" Florida State teased. "What if you were starving and I offered you a steak?"

"Or a big old sausage pizza?" Rainbow chimed in, eagerly leaning forward to clock my reaction.

"Or a three-piece dinner from Kentucky Fried Chicken?"

"I'd stick with the biscuits," I parried, slipping into my sophisticated new identity as smoothly as those New Yorkers flicked their Bics.

To tell the truth, after a long day of orientations, introductions, and shape-shifting, a sausage pizza would have hit the spot like nobody's business, but in for a penny, in for a pound. If memory serves, it was at least six years before my next taste of that former staple, though, in all frankness, you might not want to quote me on that.

Over the course of the six weeks I spent amongst the cherubim, it became second nature to request a hot dog bun with no hot dog, a practice I found surprisingly easy to keep up after the Cherub program ended. Maintaining my commitment to vegetarianism was a snap, as long as nobody witnessed me gobbling bacon bits from the salad bowl I'd been asked to carry into the dining room at home. My mother and stepfather didn't seem particularly put out by the change in my dietary habits. My appearances at the dinner table were becoming increasingly rare, eaten up by Saturday dates with James and weeknight rehearsals for *Li'l Abner.* Daddy found my vegetarianism funny, yet somehow it always managed to slip his mind between visits, so that every meal we shared, he was delighted anew. Gran-Gran was frowning but silent, still a fervent believer in the superior education and opportunities for enrichment that had unexpectedly resulted in a host of anti-Reagan proclamations, a snotty attitude toward Izod shirts, and now this.

That Thanksgiving, I granted Gran a temporary reprieve by stoically dispatching one skimpy slice of her perfectly browned bird. After that, I confined myself to stuffing, candied sweet potatoes, and plenty of surreptitious carcass picking out in the kitchen while the rest were still at the table, groaning over coffee and pie. It seemed a small concession given the nature of the holiday. Probably half of America's vegetarians were suspending their ideals in the interest of family harmony that day. For their part, my relatives kindly abstained from pointing out that the stuffing I so loved owed its succulence to the turkey juices in which it had been basted.

Sticking it to my family was hardly my primary motivation in cleaving to a vegetarian lifestyle. Impressing my peers was a far greater goal. My burger-scarfing, Izod-wearing high school friends tolerated my vegetarianism as just more semiamusing, mildly irritating fallout from my interest in theater, like *Rocky*

Horror and tattered vintage clothing. I was a showoff, but I was their showoff.

When we ordered pizza, they were more than happy to field my unwanted pepperonis, balking only if I licked my fingers before, rather than after, redistribution was accomplished. Knowing that their McNuggets would be battling my fries for dipping rights, they requested extra tubs of honey and hot mustard sauce at McDonald's. (When *Fast Food Nation* revealed that those spuds were fried in beef tallow throughout the '80s, I realized that it wasn't just the dipping sauces that were helping my fries to taste like those little felted chicken scraps. Also, that I might never have been a vegetarian in my life.)

For my eighteenth birthday, Gub-Gub gave me a copy of *The Vegetarian Epicure,* inscribed, "That's you 'n' James on the front!" How flattering to think that my skinny, Big Mac–addicted boyfriend and I could be mistaken for the idealized vegetarian lovers gracing the cover, the woman barefoot and crowned in greenery, the man lolling seductively with a big stalk of celery. The first few recipes I tried were uniformly repulsive, but that book sure looked groovy next to all those Park Tudor Chronicles on my shelf. It also supplied an articulate excuse for passing on the pork chops.

"Good food is a celebration of life," the author declares in the introduction, "and it seems absurd to me that in celebrating life we should take life." I loved the piousness of this statement so much that I found myself willing to overlook the decided nongoodness of her broccoli mousse. Given that I'd spent the last nine months believing I was a vegetarian, it was no great leap to start spouting rhetoric like some sort of long-haired, rhododendron-wreathed Joan of Arc. Of course I would battle on behalf of my voiceless animal brethren. No sacrifice was too great for them, the way it would have been if meat were made out of chocolate.

Despite growing up in Indiana, I'd never really had much interaction with livestock or, for that matter, people who knew them pre–shrink wrap. The stiff-dungareed 4-H kids winning state fair ribbons for their bottle-fed lambs didn't attend schools where grace was conducted in French. While they were slopping their hogs and gathering eggs, I was attending Saturday morning classes at Junior Civic Theater. My view of the barnyard was informed chiefly by *Charlotte's Web* and an oft-told anecdote regarding Uncle Zibah, Gran's youngest brother, who owned some sort of little farm down in Florida.

We had swung by there once on our way to Disney World. I retained a vague impression of leaning over a metal fence to pet a black-and-white cow named Lucy. (It's probably just wishful star-fucking, given Lucy's pivotal role in the upcoming anecdote.) My great-aunt and great-uncle had been raising her for however long one raises a cow, and during this time Aunt Frances developed unusually fond feelings for the beast. Frances, no stranger to the realities of farm living, had never succumbed to sentimentality when other four-legs in her care were carted off to the slaughterhouse. But when Lucy's number came up, "wall, old Frances here cried like a baby," Uncle Zibah drawled. "She carried on so, I finally had to call up and say, 'Looky here, my wife's going to pieces. If it's not too late, could you go ahead and hold off on that heifer I brung you? Her name's Lucy, and I'm coming to get her.'" It was a total Hollywood ending. Granted a permanent reprieve, Lucy ended up living the life of Riley on the farm in Florida, until she expired of natural causes at a ripe old age.

As a child, I had always imagined that given the opportunity, I, too, would have snatched Lucy from the jaws of death. Going veggie was like saving all the Lucys, or at least refraining from blatantly eating them. At that point, I'd yet to taste the delicious medallions of their babies.

It's always a shock when a vegetarian of my steely resolve falls off the wagon. Still, the flesh, as they say, is weak, and these Irish guys I met in Munich offered to treat me to Wienerschnitzel when I was too broke to buy *beer*, let alone food. Far from filling me with remorse over what could have easily remained a simple one-night stand, the experience unleashed something primal. I felt like the ex-smoker who scotches half a decade's abstinence by declaring, "You know what? Fuck cigarettes. I'm going straight to freebasing." Like the Big Bad Wolf's, my dreams were vivid with dancing sausages. If it was cured, I craved it. I was delighted to learn that during my absence, scientists had developed a whole new bacon out of turkey. I couldn't get enough of it! I devoured it straight out of the package, incapable of waiting the five minutes it was supposed to spend in the skillet.

"What?" I'd chuff around the slice hanging out of my mouth, whenever some boyfriend, up to and including the one I married, pulled an expression of disgust. "Jeez! Shnot like ish raw! See what it shesh on the label: 'Thish product ish precooked'!"

Mmm, what I wouldn't have given for another crack at a Gnaw

Bone breakfast! This time I'd have bypassed the Pop-Tarts to pile breakfast meats on up to the rafters.

Yes, I felt the occasional twinge that I was no longer celebrating life according to the parameters laid out in *The Vegetarian Epicure*, but I reminded myself that there were plenty of high school ideals I'd done well to leave by the wayside. What if my knowledge of the flesh had never been allowed to progress beyond James? Things that had seemed so fated at eighteen, in my twenties were hard to imagine. Sacrificing variety would have meant sacrificing experience—a poor choice, I thought, for one determined to make a go of it in the arts. Having experienced vegetarianism, I felt professionally obliged to go hog wild on the meaty treats I'd spent half a decade publicly rejecting.

All five senses came into play as I wandered the neighborhood like an out-of-control stray, slobbering over the Swedish butcher's sausages and every delicious aroma issuing from a back-alley vent or barbeque grill. It got so bad, even the scent of burning leaves activated my salivary glands. The rotten stench of the *carniceria* in back of the produce market was troublesome, but only for the amount of time it took to buy bananas.

Like many lapsed vegetarians, I did have several practicing vegetarian friends, most of whom had been meat-free since high school, just as I would have been (kind of) had I not encountered those Irishmen. Some of them maintained fairly militant standards regarding honey, milk, and shoe leather, but even the hardest of the hardcore seemed disinclined to hold my fall from grace against me, the way they held it against me when, say, they returned from vacation to discover that their cats had shat all over their Pier 1 Papasan chairs as a result of my failing to stick to a regular litter box–scooping schedule. Having been there myself, I could hardly begrudge them the pleasure they took in taunting me with talk of lips, anuses, and other assorted hot dog yummies. It was all in good fun.

Besides, I wasn't a total philistine. I knew my PETA literature. I was opposed to blinding bunnies and electrocuting monkeys. I hated that falsely folksy Frank Perdue just as much as they did. There's something evil about a fortune made on poultry ordered de-beaked and de-legged long before they're slated to go to chicken heaven. Given my already well-informed status, the "education" my downstairs neighbor and theatrical cohort Dave delighted in subjecting me to was really just one of those comedy routines that develop over the course of a long and comfortable friendship.

"Do you know how chickens are raised in this country?" he'd inquire from time to time, usually when we were hanging around our theater's lobby with carryout from Andy's or the nearby Middle Eastern grocery.

"Fecal soup?" I'd smile. Fecal soup was a subject Dave held particularly dear.

"That's right, fecal soup!" he'd cry happily, his teeth bared in the same rictus of triumph the lioness exhibits, raising her bloody muzzle from the flank of her kill. "American chickens spend their entire lives in these wire cages, positioned an inch or so above their water supply. Which they also defecate in. So when they drink, they're drinking their own feces. It'd be like you or me drinking out of the toilet."

That part always slayed me. My stepfather had a black Lab who habitually nosed his way into the downstairs powder room for a big, sloppy drink, so much so that one of the first things my mother told company was always, "And if you have to go to the bathroom, be sure and close the lid." I was totally in love with the idea of some unsuspecting theater patron asking directions to the facilities, only to stumble in on me or Dave lapping noisily from the commode.

"It's true though, you know. And I'm not the one who made up that phrase 'fecal soup.' That's how it's referred to in the industry."

"So you've mentioned."

"So when you're biting into that *souvlaki* you have there, just take a moment to think 'fecal soup.'"

"I always do."

Dave had my number, all right. Like many young carnivores trying to make a go of it in the low-budget arts scene, I consumed a disproportionate amount of poultry. Professional chefs may sniff that chicken is the least exciting flesh to work with, but it's inexpensive, easy to prepare and—have you heard?—drinks its own shit! What's not to love? It didn't even need a recipe, just a pan, some olive oil, some garlic, a little bit of salt, maybe a splash of white wine or some lemon juice. Nothing smelled better on the stove, especially when it was steaming up the windows on a cold winter afternoon. It made me feel like a nineteenth-century French peasant, the sexy, robust kind who uses a lot of rosemary from the garden and doesn't require a glass for her *vin ordinaire.* Presumably that same peasant would have had to engage in some strangling and plucking before she could take up her fork, but not me. I could barely handle looking at the rubber chicken we kept backstage. The actual anatomy of meat was something I preferred not to consider, until I dissected a human cadaver, that is.

It was a great experience, actually, particularly for someone studying massage therapy as a means of supplementing a lowly theatrical income, but it kind of freaked me out that some part of me wanted to try a little nibble. The urge was far from bloodthirsty. I mean, it's not like I was going to rip off a foot and stuff it in my mouth. I wouldn't have had to, since this particular cadaver lab put beginners at ease by keeping the dead bodies under wraps until we'd each had a chance to examine a severed foot, which the work-study students carried out on orange plastic lunch trays identical to the ones at Wendy's. Next up were brains, which I found about as appetizing as clay. Wild horses couldn't have induced me to eat them.

Then we uncovered our cadavers. Most of them seemed fairly fresh, plump with formaldehyde, not creepy as I'd feared, just sort of naked and dead. The one to which I'd been assigned, however, looked like he'd been hanging around for a while. I was not the first to have a go at him, a work-study student explained. Before hooking up with me, my cadaver had participated in a thoracic cavity seminar and had had his nerves "dissected out" by an aspiring chiropractor. His musculoskeletal system remained intact, though, making him an appropriate match for me.

The fact that I'd been given someone else's leftovers didn't bother me in the slightest. On the contrary, I found it quite beautiful that no piece of him would be wasted. The only problem was, he had gotten so dried out that he was starting to resemble my grandmother's pot roast. His flesh had a well-done appearance. Every muscle my scalpel probed flaked along the grain so readily that the lack of mashed potatoes seemed like an oversight. If he'd been laid out on damask instead of stainless steel, I'd have popped a sliver in my mouth without giving it a second thought. Just a sneaky little vegetarian-on-Thanksgiving taste. I was dying to ask one of the cute work-study boys if he ever felt similarly inclined toward cannibalism but, not wanting to seem a ghoul, limited myself to inquiring if he'd ever seen *Dawn of the Dead,* and if so, did he ever think about it when he was alone in the storage room, inventorying the latest shipment.

My close call in the cadaver lab didn't put an end to my carnivorous ways, though the heightened grasp of anatomy that I walked with made me uncomfortably aware of tendon and sinew, even in the boneless, skinless breasts I continued to prepare any number of ways. In terms of connective tissue, a chicken is basically no different from a human, a fact that kept reasserting itself as I marbled—excuse me, massaged—the oily flesh of friends and family eagerly clamoring to serve as my guinea pigs. Still, the common yard bird was too tasty, too indispensable to my current celebration of life, to do away with just like that. I cut back a bit when Greg and I moved to New York City, settling into an East Village tenement just a half block from First Avenue Meat Products, but only because I considered it my civic duty to partake of the locally produced kielbasa several times a week.

Remarkably, most of my new East Coast friends and acquaintances assumed I was vegetarian. I don't know if it was the massage thing, the hippie dress printed with dancing Shivas, or the fact that I still dabbled in tofu, but something about me must have screamed "herbivore." In an ironic twist, I now felt compelled to give prospective hosts and hostesses a courtesy call to apprise them of my lack of dietary restrictions. "Really? You're not vegan?" my hostess-to-be would ask in surprise.

"No, I eat everything," I'd assure her.

"Listen, it's no trouble to make you an omelet. Are you lacto-ovo?"

"Uh, I always forget, is that the one where you don't eat dairy or you don't eat anything but dairy?"

"So, wait, you do eat dairy, then?"

"Yes, but you don't have to make me an omelet. I mean, unless that's what everybody else is having."

"Are you sure? It's really no trouble. Or, I know, if you don't like eggs, I could whip you up some plain pasta, not plain-plain, just without the meat."

"That's okay. To tell you the truth, I hate pasta." Dead silence. I should have told her I was gluten intolerant. People who gladly accommodate outside-the-mainstream guests by braising an acorn squash in homemade mushroom stock often turn frosty when I make the tactical error of revealing my un-American feelings toward everyone's favorite dish. And sadly, these days, I find myself in a position where I must choke down a fair amount of it.

It's my own damn fault for renouncing meat yet again. I didn't climb all the way back into the wagon; I'm sort of hanging on to the running board with a bag full of fish. The reasons behind this latest change of heart are pretty boring and difficult to support, particularly when one is talking to a lobster or a trout. Suffice it to say that once again, I'm a nightmare to invite to dinner, there's very little for me to order in Peruvian restaurants, and if the vegetarians who don't eat fish choose to write me off as an irritating wannabe, they're well within their rights. About once a week I find myself at an ethical crossroads, wondering whether to cross-examine a Chinatown waiter about the broth in which my veggie noodles will float or give up the charade and tell him to bring me some pork fried rice. After all, it's not like he knows anyone I know, and either way, I'll probably end up eating pork.

But just as I'm about to chuck it all, I think of the piglet, Babe, crying "Mom?" as a load of curly-tailed, apparently non-English-speaking extras are herded off to the abattoir, and I realize I'm no longer equipped to be so brazen. Jesus Christ, is this what having kids does to you? Now when people ask if I'm vegetarian, my answer is neither the earthy "Used to be" of my hickory-smoked idyll, nor the resounding, duplicitous "Yes!" of early adulthood. I question the morality of dunking lobsters—or "insects of the sea" as Greg calls them—into boiling water while still sentient (the lobsters, that is), yet sometimes can't resist ordering them in special occasion restaurants where the only other option that fits my constraints is a fifteen-dollar plate of Seasonal Steamed Crudité. (Mussels and swordfish ceased to be options when Anthony Bourdain let it leak that they're stored in their own piss and riddled with giant worms, respectively.)

"Why don't you just tell people you're a pescetarian?" a vegetarian I met recently asked, cutting me off midapologia for my beat-up leather jacket and my callow habit of behaving as if fish are neurologically no more complex than eggplants. Was he kidding? Or was this his passive-aggressive way of letting me know that, as far as he was concerned, I was full of fecal soup? No, he was serious. "It means someone who eats fish," he clarified.

Maybe so, but why bother with a label so few can define? Especially when "basket case" is just as accurate, while still leaving lots of wiggle room for the future.

chipotle chili

Customize it to suit any palate: carnivorous, white meat only, pescetarian, vegetarian, cannibalistic . . . the chipotle ensures that modifications of the flesh won't lead to culinary ruination.

Prepare 20 tomatillos for takeoff by husking their papery skins, rinsing off the resin, coring the stems, and chopping them into quarters.

Chop a large onion and sauté it in some olive oil, right in the stockpot's big old heavy bottom.

When the onion smells wonderful, add the tomatillos, a lime's worth of lime juice, and 6 crushed garlic cloves.

Cook them for 10 minutes, giving things a stir every now and again.

While the veggies are reducing themselves to a delicious sludge, kick salmonella to the curb by cooking whatever meat, fish, or fowl you plan on chucking into the pot. I used to make it with a ½ lb of turkey sausage, plooped out of its casing. Now I make it with an equivalent amount of shrimp or some unholy approximation from the fake-meat store in Chinatown. When eating higher on the food chain, please be sure that shit is done, and remember that there's a reason why organic tastes better and costs more. Thus concludeth the sermon. Into the pot it goes!

Now add:

- 1 big can of white beans, rinsed of the slimy stuff
- 1 big can of black beans, also rinsed (better safe than sorry)
- ½ bunch of cilantro, leaves and stems, chopped
- 1 jar of salsa, preferably green

another lime's worth of lime juice

a couple dashes of the vinegar of your choice

1 chopped canned chipotle pepper (or, for a burning ring of fire, 2)

Bring it to a boil, simmer as long or as little as you like to achieve the desired consistency, and serve with sour cream and warm corn tortillas.

what are the odds?

The lobster dinner St. Vincent's offers all new mothers served as my introduction to hospital dining. In my case, the fancy meal was not so much a victory banquet as a consolation prize for the unexpected complications that earned me an unwanted mid-labor transfer from the groovy, freestanding birthing center where I'd planned to deliver in a hot tub.

The Seton Center's midwives kept a sheaf of delivery menus on file, an array diverse enough to satisfy every possible permutation of postpartum cravings. I hadn't worked out in advance which West Village restaurant would receive the pleasure of my patronage. The sentimental choice would have been Mama Buddha, a healthful and high-ceilinged Chinese place on the corner of 11th and Hudson. I'd gotten into the habit of capping every prenatal appointment with a plate of their brown rice and Stir-Fried Green Leafy Mixed Vegetable. It must have been a popular item, since the waitresses seemed to spend all their downtime seated around a circular table, sorting through a towering heap of difficult-to-identify vegetal material that was, as advertised, leafy, mixed, and green. These young ladies had followed my pregnancy with such sporting interest, I wanted them to be among the first to learn of the baby's arrival. The delivery boy would remember to deliver my glad tidings if I made it worth his while.

The Cowgirl Hall of Fame was another nearby contender. Mama Buddha's light fare had been perfectly suited to the diminished stomach space of the final trimester, but perhaps pushing that baby out was an effort best rewarded with a pulled-pork sandwich and a margarita. If their ice cream "baked potatoes" traveled well, I might order a couple of those, too.

Of course, if it was a gut bomb I was craving, the Sucelt Coffee Shop's dirt-cheap *comida latina* was so near at hand that I could probably skip the delivery boy altogether and just toddle a few doors down with my newborn babe in my arms. The mere thought of a big, squashy $3.75 Sucelt Cubana, oozing pickles and melted cheese, set me all aslobber, but I was determined to keep my options open so I could be truly spontaneous when the big moment arrived. Perhaps I'd find myself hankering after Indian or Thai or Greek.

Whichever way I might have leapt, it's a sure bet I wouldn't have celebrated with a lobster. If I'm being hit up for "market price," I expect something grander than a Styrofoam clamshell leaking brownish fluid onto a half ream of flimsy Bev-Naps. In my humble opinion, that kind of scratch merits cloth napkins, expert service, flattering lighting, and the opportunity to show oneself off in something dressier than a hospital gown and a belted sanitary pad the size of a twin mattress.

Granted, St Vincent's lobster was free, but I'd really been looking forward to the whole delivery ritual, the fumbling for the wallet, the transfer of the toasty bags, the decision to mark the occasion with a larger-than-usual tip. What a fine way it would have been to initiate the next generation into the wonders of big-city living. Instead, we got an enthusiastic cabbie who actually seemed to be rooting for the baby to crown in his backseat during the two-block ride that constituted my emergency transfer from the birthing center to the hospital, and a peon in cafeteria-colored surgical scrubs unceremoniously bearing my one-size-fits-all victory dinner to my bedside on a plastic lunch tray.

"Uh, doesn't he get one, too?" I asked, nodding at Greg, who slumped in a ripped vinyl armchair, totally beat. The deliverer reached beneath the gauze mushroom cap that covered her hair and scratched the top of her ear.

"Did he just have a baby?" she smirked. I shook my head.

"Uh-uh, that's right, Mommy. To get the lobster, you got to do the work!" As soon as she'd taken her leave, I peeked beneath the nubbly thermal plastic dome. What I saw bore a closer resemblance to cat food than the crustacean of kings. The melted butter was starting to congeal, and in place of champagne, I'd been given a wee dram of apple juice with a peel-back foil lid. Yuck. If these were the spoils of motherhood, Greg was welcome to them.

Following tradition, the minute I'd found out I was pregnant, I'd dutifully swapped my three daily cappuccinos for a grain-based hot beverage composed primarily of barley and toasted beets. (Well, first I went to Two Boots on Avenue A to gird my loins with a Mel Cooley—sun-dried tomatoes, pesto, ricotta, and roast peppers on a thin crust—washed down with a boot-shaped glass vessel of beer, but just one, okay? One.)

Henceforth, I adhered to what is known to millions of expectant American mothers as the "Best Odds Diet," a tyrannical nutritional checklist that reawakened in me the long-dormant horror

I used to experience whenever my mother told me to stop making faces and eat my beef Stroganoff.

I had nothing against most of the Best Choice Foods the authors of the Diet had anointed with their particularly off-putting brand of self-righteous zeal—the almond butter, the whole-grain bread, the alfalfa and canned salmon. Not anymore. Twenty years earlier, I'd balked at most of what I was expected to eat, but now my greatest umbrage was reserved for what I was expected not to eat. No aioli, no feta, no wine, no sugar? Dag. How was I supposed to make cold sesame noodles if homemade mayo had been classified verboten?

It sucked, but, gritting my teeth, I abided, scared that the slightest deviation from the path signposted BEST would result in a resentful and underweight cyclops baby with a vestigial tail. I did without Caesar salad, rare meat, and, most egregiously, sushi. I limited myself to Virgin Marys in East Village pubs whose Guinness-centric decor served as constant torment. For nine months, my unpasteurized-cheese holes went empty as I choked back nettles for iron, raspberry leaves to ripen my uterus, and five to seven daily servings of whole grains. Follow this regimen, the literature implied, and you'll have a healthy baby. Oh yeah? Here's what cleaving to those excellent Odds got me: seven hours of pushing, a vaginal hematoma, and a seriously fucked up baby who spent the first couple weeks of her life in the neonatal intensive care unit. Okay, so maybe leafy greens and lack of coffee weren't entirely to blame, but sitting beside Inky's NICU bassinet, between an abandoned preemie and a couple of shrieking crack babies, I couldn't help feeling that there'd been some mistake.

Inky eventually pulled through, but two years later, when I found myself up the stick again, I had very little patience left for lectures about what "Mommy" could and couldn't eat to ensure her child the best possible start in life. I didn't plan to wash down raw oysters with Dewar's anytime soon, but damned if I'd let some layette-happy pregnancy manual boss me around. Pregnant with Inky, I had looked and felt like a million bucks. (Just for the record, anyone who attributes this to my oat straw–heavy, caffeine-and-alcohol-free diet does so at risk of having his or her face ripped off the next time we meet.) This go-round, it was as if some fiend had siphoned off my blood and replaced it with embalming fluid. Chalk it up to morning sickness or the effects of nursing a toddler while a bun's in the oven, but I was one wan chickie. Intuition told me that making it to the end zone depended on regular infusions of coffee, beer, and ice cream. (The latter isn't contraindicated for fetal health, just models, movie stars, and those figure-conscious Strollercizers who'll be snapping up their size twos within three days of giving birth anyway.)

My Good-Enough Odds Diet might not have cut the mustard with the pregnancy gurus, but it seemed to agree with my soon-to-be-baby, whom an ultrasound revealed to be a boy, or possibly a girl with an ear of baby corn between her legs. By the final trimester, I was feeling pretty good, too, as the low-level nausea that had ushered in the millennium gave way to something resembling my vitality of old. Once again, I could bop between Coney Island, the East Village, the Upper West Side, and Chinatown, hauling Inky on the subway along with umpteen bags of groceries, which I then hauled up three flights, an Amazon with a watermelon concealed in her overalls. I felt as strapping as one of those pioneers who acted as their own midwives when their water broke in the fields. I fully expected the stork to find me on my feet, engaged in some urban, latter-day hoeing equivalent. Fortified by hops, sweetened creams, cured meats, and the rich black snakes of espresso roast, I sailed toward my due date, confident that this time, nothing would go awry.

Alas, sometime in my eighth month, I was whipping up a stove-spatteringly delicious pot of Middling Odds that taste good with beer and leave curry stains on everything they come into contact with, when someone snuck up behind me and clobbered me over the head with a two-by-four. That's what it felt like, anyway. One second, I was bending down to retrieve a couple of runaway chickpeas, and the next, *whammo!* I was crawling toward the bedroom on all fours, whimpering like a wounded animal who needs to lie down for a few minutes before putting dinner on the table.

This was not the first time I'd been tempted to do so, of course, but it was the first time I'd succumbed, probably because my brain was threatening to kick a hole in my occipital ridge. I lay there in the dark, wondering if, subconsciously, the only thing I was sick with was the desire to put on a show. Maybe all I wanted was the coddling I'd be assured were I to develop gestational diabetes or preeclampsia, just a quick nibble of bed rest before picking up where I'd left off.

After a while, Greg came in and asked if I wanted him to turn on the lights. I did not. He asked if he should make some spaghetti. I nodded without opening my eyes. He asked if I would like some. No, but perhaps the razor-fanged space leech who'd attached itself to my medulla oblongata would after it was finished with me.

I swear to god, that was the longest night of my life, longer even than the one passed three years earlier in a birthing suite of the Elizabeth Seton Childbearing Center, where Greg, Little MoMo, and a full complement of midwives, nurses, and student nurses kept telling me that my baby would be out before sunrise, as if saying so often enough might somehow make it true. Then I'd at least had a general idea of what was happening to my body, why it hurt so bad. The storm I was currently weathering felt like a nightmare acid trip in a bad '60s movie, complete with psychedelic dissolves, crazy-ass zooms, and a disturbing soundtrack.

You know that song from *The Music Man*, the one where all the townspeople line up to sing about how there's nothing halfway about the Iowa way to yadda-yadda-whatever and then they list half the goddamn towns in the motherfucking Hawkeye State? *Oughta give Iowa a try*, that one? I couldn't get it out of my head. If pain hadn't pinned me to the bed, I'd have hurled myself out the window, just to make it stop. It got so bad that I found myself trying to recall the lyrics to "Marian the Librarian," "Gary, Indiana"—anything that might lead to a detour from Dubuque, Des Moines, Davenport, Marshalltown, Mason City, Keokuk, Ames, Clear Lake . . . At six in the morning, I cried uncle, nudging Greg awake to beg him to drive me to the emergency room.

I was resigned to do my time in the waiting-room chairs, but the triage nurse took one look at me shivering in my ragged quilt from home and ushered me to the back, where

I shivered on a hospital bed, mostly unattended, for another ten or so hours. At one point, the other bed was occupied by a woman who offered to get me some Tylenol, even though she could barely walk, she was so eaten up by sickle-cell anemia. A couple of rooms down, a kid with a broken leg pelted the doctor with obscenities and, when that didn't work, wailed piteously for his mommy. Another woman stormed the halls, telling anyone who would listen that the hospital was discriminating against black people and people with AIDS by denying her pain medication. "And," she spat, sticking her head into our darkened room, "I work here!"

"What you bothering these ladies for?" a nurse hollered, squeaking down the corridor in her big Jet-Puffed shoes. "Didn't I tell you to stay in that room until the doctor come?"

"Fuck you, bitch! How many times I need to tell you that I need me some goddamn pain management?"

"You want pain management? Fine. Call patient services and tell it to them because I cannot authorize—"

"Damn straight I want me some fucking pain management!"

"There is the phone! Call them! Be my guest!"

"I'm nobody's 'guest,' bitch! I work here!"

Wow. Compared to her, I felt remarkably palliated, grateful just to be exempted from the insurmountable challenge of preparing Inky's breakfast. Three years of shattered sleep, nursing, and hauling the kid on public transit had done a number on my poor old body. I tell you, naptimes are wasted on the young. I was no trouble at all, curled up as quietly as a kitten, praying that I didn't have meningitis.

Symptoms-wise, I recognized myself as a textbook case:

fever, a blinding headache, and a beyond-stiff neck, not to mention vomiting and "whimpering in a high-pitched tone." This last is generally associated with infants, but let us not forget that I was nearly nine months pregnant. Scary, yes, but I'd been trained to remain patient in the belief that eventually, good behavior is rewarded with the appropriate medical treatment and a pack of Fruit Stripe gum or a small plastic toy. Maybe I'd get me another lobster.

Fortunately, exhaustion, both physical and mental, prevented me from dwelling on how the staff seemed to have relegated me to a permanent back burner, or how this guy Greg worked with knew a guy whose girlfriend got meningitis and died, all within a twenty-four-hour period. What I really needed was an advocate, someone not afraid to make waves to get satisfaction, someone like my old housemate Randall. He would have known how to handle Dr. Spinal Tap, whose bedside manner, when he finally arrived, clanged with an exasperated certainty in his own intellectual superiority. Because I couldn't lay on my belly, he directed me to sit on the edge of the bed with the back of my gown opened.

"Bend over more," he snapped, pushing roughly on my shoulder in an attempt to fold me over my distended abdomen. "No, more! More!" Perhaps when he went to med school, full-term fetuses were collapsible. I don't know. "Bend all the way! More! To your lap!"

"She can't," the med student helping to support me in my seated position murmured sympathetically, if inaudibly.

"Oh, this is stupid!" the doc shouted. "I give up! How can I find a good place to stick the needle when she is so fat?"

Fat? Fuck him! I wasn't fat; I was nearly nine months

pregnant! If ever there was a time I was supposed to be fat, this was it! Who did he expect? Kate Moss? Too bad he wasn't an OB. He could have put his patients on an Even Better Odds Diet, one where they'd eat nothing but lettuce and dryer lint! If I weren't so worried that I'd end up like Willie's friend's girlfriend, I'd have taken him down, this misanthropic, Orwellian nightmare of a neurologist with his imperious Old World accent and his case full of syringes, one of which he stabbed without the slightest warning into my big fat back and great balls of fire, did that hurt like a back-alley organ harvest in the furnaces of hell! Having drawn off several agonizing vials of clear fluid, he returned from the lab to tell me that the samples were unusable. *Oh mother of god. Just kill me now. Kill me, and confine me to an afterlife in which I'm locked in a hotel room with Andy-Panda, or Mrs. Hogarth, or a giant tureen of girl crap, because really, how could it be any worse than this?*

"No, just kidding," Dr. Tap chuckled, enjoying his little joke. "You are a very brave girl. And we're going to admit you."

Against my will, I smiled. I was happy because something was really wrong with me. My white blood cells were most definitely out of whack. No doubt Dr. Tap had thought I was faking.

It was a toss-up as to whether I had bacterial or viral meningitis, so the doctors decided to treat me for the more serious of the two by putting me on IV antibiotics and quarantine. A maternity nurse was supposed to swing by to monitor the baby's heartbeat every couple of hours, but this plan petered out after a mere two appearances. Other than Greg and our friends, who were circumscribed by hospital visiting hours, the only people I saw with any regularity were the guy who showed up every morning to see if I wanted the television turned on and the cafeteria folk. They'd drop off the next day's menu with dinner, and it's a sad comment on the way time passes in a hospital that I perused it with relish.

I liked imagining how Chicken Florentine with Vegetable Medley and Roll would taste under more favorable culinary circumstances, perhaps on a snowy evening in some endearingly unfashionable West Village restaurant, the kind of place where you might order port or run into Calvin Trillin, who's been going there every Wednesday night since 1952, when he rhapsodized about the Florentine in the pages of the *New Yorker.* Hmm, maybe I should have authorized that man to turn on my TV. It's pathetic how much entertainment I wrung from the mere act of indicating my preference for coffee or tea, creamy Italian or vinaigrette, fruit cocktail or canned peaches, considering carefully before checking the appropriate box. This aspect of patient experience ran parallel to an airplane passenger's. Even if the grub wasn't worth looking forward to, the hubbub surrounding it was. I reckon it's the same when mealtime rolls around in prison.

"How we doing today?" the cafeteria lady sang out through the gauze mask everyone (except the doctors) was required to don upon entering my room. She was such a warm, easygoing presence; none of that "Hi, my name's Patti and I'll be your server!" perkiness that so jangles the nerves.

"Doing great!" I smiled, throwing down my book and sitting right up as a signal of receptivity, should a recitation of daily specials be forthcoming. It never was, but as a former waitress, I'm bound to extend professional courtesy to my brethren, no matter how degraded the venue. It wasn't the cafeteria lady's fault that the tray smelled like doody. Lowering the safety bars, she wheeled my little faux-wood typing table into position above my outstretched legs, while I continued to beam up at her, leeching as much enjoyment from the interaction as I possibly could. "How are you doing?"

My friend grunted humorously, which I understood as a sort of shorthand for her varicose veins, her shitty job, and the heat wave raging outside the hospital walls. Then the rack of trays she had left just outside the door beckoned, and I was left alone with a big old ice cream scoop of Park Tudor–style reconstituted mashed potatoes.

Truth was, I was actually okay for food. Owing to the proximity of Sahadi's, a famed New York grocery whose bulk bins are the stuff of legend, the bottom drawer of my nightstand was stocked with enough dried fruit, nuts, and chocolate-covered raisins to sustain half the rats in the subway system. With a stash like that, I could afford to turn my nose up at breakfast, lunch, and dinner, but boy, was I starving for company. In my twenties, I volunteered to deliver meals on wheels to homebound people with AIDS. It always haunted me how sad the recipients looked when I re-zipped my red insulated vinyl bag of dwindling, aluminum-wrapped, reheatable entrées and bid them goodbye.

Oh, come on! They won't miss you. They don't even know you! I told myself, rationalizing that the only things the people on my list were pining for were their health and a return to the days when our base of operations was a wildly popular Swedish diner in Boys' Town. That joint's sausages and cinnamon rolls could have taken the gold in the postcoital Olympics, had the establishment not been disqualified on grounds of extreme cleanliness. It was the most sanitary setup I'd ever seen, but it ain't public health if it's not completely bungled, so some official determined that our clients' nutritional needs would be better served if the contract was transferred to the kitchen of a nearby hospital. Like AIDS isn't punishment enough! Attempting to raise volunteer morale after this ill-advised venue change, our supervisor insisted that the human contact we provided was its own form of sustenance, a hypothesis I was now equipped to buy into.

Around sunrise on the fifth day, a nurse padded in, hooked me up to the antiquated Hewlett-Packard baby monitor we all made fun of, returned a few minutes later to check the printout, and started screaming for transport. In less time than it takes to fill an ice cube tray, she had me on a gurney, racing pell-mell toward the elevators, nurses and orderlies running alongside. It was so much like a scene from *ER*, if I hadn't been so terrified, I know I would have enjoyed the hell out of it.

"What's happening?" I screamed, struggling to sit up.

"We have to get the baby out!" the main nurse shouted as we rounded the corner into some sort of abattoir where my pubic hair was unceremoniously scraped off with a Daisy razor, a catheter got shoved up where the sun don't shine, and an unconnected IV speared the back of my hand so forcefully, a juice glass's worth of blood hit the floor with a big liquid *splat*. What I wouldn't have given to be back in my room, prodding a rectangle of prefab hash browns with a spork. I wondered if I'd ever see my chocolate raisins again. Greg came racing in, looking like he'd just rolled out of bed, which indeed he had. Behind him was a white-coated obstetrician, who, compared to everyone else, seemed remarkably calm, chomping nonchalantly on a stick of Doublemint.

"How ya doin'?" he asked.

"Uh," I said.

"Who ordered this?" he frowned, unfurling the baby monitor printout clipped to my chart. I couldn't help gloating that the main nurse sounded defensive, enumerating her reasons. The doctor listened, then winked at me. "Let's not do anything rash," he smiled. *Amen to that, brother.* "Okay, I'm going to go grab some coffee." The nurses cleaned up, then cleared out.

"Jeezums," Greg observed. He recounted the events of the last hour as they had transpired on his end, the mad dash to leave Inky at the home of some playground friends, then make it to the hospital before they cut me open. I rang for the nurse. "Um, do you think they're still planning to give me a C-section? Because my husband needs to feed the meter, but he doesn't want to miss anything."

"I think that'd be okay," she whispered with a kind and conspiratorial smile.

"Really? Well, then, let me ask you, in your opinion, are we pushing it if he swings by Taco Bell?"

*

In short order, I was moved to a new room on the maternity ward, where the presence of a roommate suggested that I'd been taken off quarantine. Actually, it was more like ten roommates, since the pregnant sixteen-year-old in the other bed came surrounded by a boisterous coterie of friends and family who'd turned her half of the room into a sort of clubhouse. Ravenous for human interaction, I readied myself to join the club, but before introductions could be made, my roomie's mom yanked the vinyl curtain between our beds closed without a word.

Rejected, I lay there eavesdropping on the merrymakers, the loudest of whom was, by a nose, Dr. Sally Jessy Raphael. The door kept slamming as callers came and went, often on a mission to procure or deliver refreshments. This was difficult for me, as the *chalupas* Greg had fetched a couple of hours earlier had left me raring for more salt and grease. My friend Anna had called to say she'd be swinging by after work with an assortment of vegetarian sushi from the East Village, but even the promise of this treat could not stop me from coveting what my roommate's crew was so lustily savoring.

I couldn't see them, but oh lord, I could hear them. And smell them. It was a total throwback to the first time I fell off the vegetarian wagon. I thought I'd swoon when one newcomer surfed in atop a great aromatic wave of Kentucky Fried Chicken. The Best Odds authors would have likely pointed to the Colonel as the reason my roomie was leaking amniotic fluid like a faucet, two months before she was due to deliver, but I have to say, my mouth was watering. Back in my meals-on-wheels-for-people-with-AIDS days, whenever I'd find myself feeling blue, I'd buy myself a three-piece dinner and eat it on my bed, watching a tape of *Easy Rider* or alternatively, *Mister Rogers*. Best therapy I ever had.

"What's this damn Original Recipe shit?" complained a youthful, female voice on the other side of the curtain. "I told Dante to tell you Extra Crispy!"

"Don't start," an older-sounding woman retorted, indignant but also weirdly jocular. "No ma'am! Don't y'all be starting in on me after the day I've had! That bitch principal called me in to school, saying Dante hit his teacher or some such. I said, 'Bitch, I'd have hit her too!'" The relatives' cries of delight were borne aloft on the fizzy *kachunks* of a half dozen soda cans opening simultaneously. "Bitch said she was going to call security on my ass!"

And then they popped open the chips, and I thought I would lose my mind. I love chips of all kinds, sour cream 'n' onion, salt and vinegar, barbeque, and oh, sweet Jesus, Pringles, but I also react, well, phobically to the sound of other people eating them. It's the crunching. I can be sitting in a movie theater, wholly absorbed in the film, when *zoop*, the veil lifts and I become painfully aware of my fellow patrons' jaws moving up and down, gnashing away at an endless supply of popcorn. It's like being surrounded by giant mantises and their clicking, sideways mandibles. I have to bite the heel of my hand to keep from screaming.

Greg insists it's pure obnoxiousness on my part, but I swear to god, it's a genuine, if undiagnosed, affliction. I don't know if I'm the only sufferer, if there are others whom Audible Cheeto Eating Syndrome causes to grapple blindly with their coat buttons and shoelaces, frantic to get away from anything binding. I can tell you that it's something my fancy education left me ill equipped to deal with, particularly in a situation such as this. I can write term papers and say grace in French, but how on earth to ask my roomie and her potentially pugilistic visitors to chew more quietly without seeming prissy or, worse, inadvertently sparking a racial incident?

Pardon me, folks, I'm the uptight white woman twice this young lady's age, and if it's not too much trouble, I'm wondering if there's any chance you might consider nibbling your junk food in such a way that you don't sound like giant insects? I wouldn't dream of interfering, except I'm a stuck-up cunt. And also, while I'm thinking of it, do you think it would be all right if I helped myself to one of your drumsticks?

According to a soft-spoken infectious disease specialist with an unpronounceable last name who dropped in later that afternoon, food had been getting me into all kinds of trouble lately. The way she saw it, I *didn't* have meningitis, neither viral nor bacterial. Instead, I had something called listeria. "Do you know what that is?" she asked.

I nodded, picturing a purple-flowered vine. I was having a little trouble hearing her over the explosive *Power Rangers* adventure blaring from my roommate's eternal electronic flame. At least the chips had been exhausted.

"Good, okay, so let's say you are having some goat cheese, maybe it is okay, but maybe if you are elderly or HIV-positive or pregnant, maybe it is not so okay."

Compared to Dr. Tap, this practitioner's modest manner went down smoothly, especially in light of the day's events. Unlike Best Odds, she was capable of discussing goat cheese with a pregnant woman in a noncondescending way. She listed listeria's symptoms: headache, stiff neck, vomiting . . . they sure sounded familiar.

"So I don't have meningitis; I have wisteria? Is that why they tried to give me a C-section this morning?"

"Oh, that was just a stupid nurse." I think that's what she said. The Power Rangers were taking down a villain, and she was already halfway out of the room.

"Wait, though, can you get wisteria without eating goat cheese? Because I've been kind of relaxed about some of the things the pregnancy manuals tell you to avoid, but that's one of the ones I've steered clear of."

"No goat cheese?" I shook my head. The doctor fired off a laundry list's worth of killer cheeses, but cross my heart, I hadn't tasted any of them in nearly a year. I'd gorged myself silly on a platter of fancy *fromages* in LA three weeks earlier, but having been present when the cashier swiped them across the electric eye of my new boyfriend, Trader Joe's, I could confirm that that shit had been hard and expensive. Maybe it was the wine that had poisoned me, or too much caffeine. It couldn't have been Ben and Jerry, could it? My money was on the kale that damn pregnancy manual deified as a Best Odds choice for baby. "When you are cooking vegetables, are you washing them always?" the doctor asked.

I knew it! It was the kale. But god forbid I out myself as less-than-scrupulous kitchen help, not to this unobtrusive, tastefully coiffed specialist, this phenomenally high achiever from a country around whose perimeter I'd backpacked like some ankle-belled hippie ding-dong.

"Oh," I hedged, "I'd say I'm about average. I give them a rinse, same as anybody."

She knitted her brows, nodding. "It is important to really wash them. Because, let's say a cow is going to the bathroom. A farmer takes this manure and puts it on the soil where the vegetables are growing." Her delicacy was starting to rankle. Having spent the morning with a catheter jammed into my pee-er and my pubes in a little pile on the floor, and the afternoon bedeviled by both KFC and ACES, I would have appreciated some straight talk to clue me in to what I had, why I had it, and what, if any, was the game plan for getting me home, where I could take care of my kid, switch off the TV at will, and open a window anytime I felt like it, where no one would try to cut me open or tap my spine and the grub was light-years removed from the official meals my insurance company was being roundly bilked for, whether or not they were eaten. Before I could give voice to any of these concerns, Dr. Can'tpronounceorevenrememberit's beeper went off and she fled, pledging to have her secretary Xerox some information on my behalf.

I'm not sure why she failed to mention that listeria frequently causes stillborn babies, but in retrospect, I'm very glad no one hipped me to this tidbit until after I'd been deemed out of the woods. And the specter of poorly washed vegetables aside, we never learned for sure exactly what it was that I had ingested to land my pregnant ass in the hospital for nearly three weeks. (Both my insurance company and the hospital administrators wanted to keep me incarcerated until I gave birth, but my hero, the gum-chewing OB, finally prevailed upon the powers that be to spring me with a home IV hookup, contingent on a letter from Greg, stating that he wouldn't sue if I croaked.)

I did notice a little story in the *Times* a few weeks after Milo's miraculously complication-free delivery, about a recall by an extremely well-known New York cold-cut company, the one whose logo graces every deli case in the five boroughs, the one whose delivery trucks can be found blocking a bike lane at any given hour.

My interest piqued, I called the company's hotline, where a recorded message told me that the company was so concerned with its pregnant consumers' peace of mind, it had voluntarily recalled half its products, even though it was quite confident that its products were in no way responsible for harboring the bacteria that had recently caused a small outbreak of listeriosis in the Tri-State region. The message made no specific mention of the sliced roast beef I had taken to purchasing in my final trimester as a precaution against both anemia and the brewed nettles I had gulped down when pregnant with Inky. Man, those sandwiches hit the spot. Their memory is as close as I've ever gotten to an answer. Not being the litigious type, I can only assume that the corporate stance is sufficiently iron rich to withstand all accusations springing from something as wholesome as roast beef on rye.

watermelon with feta and basil

Essentially, I just gave you the recipe. Sounds odd, but once you taste it, you'll spend the rest of your life craving it, especially when you can't have it. Speaking of which, in the interest of public health, I encourage you to take a pregnancy test, teach the cow to differentiate between the bathroom and the basil patch, and discontinue immediately if experiencing meningitis-like symptoms.

Chop a watermelon into cubes. Dazzle your guests with one of those yellow-fleshed models that doesn't have so goddamn many seeds.

Crumble some feta cheese over the watermelon. Feta cheese is most delectable in the spring, when the herd can feed on tender, new grass . . . and hothouse watermelons are going for 5 bucks a pound.

Chop some fresh basil and throw it in there, like festive green confetti.

Experiment with your proportions to find the combination most ticklish to your own personal palate. If you demand a more scientific approach, I'd say 4 parts watermelon, 1 part feta, and ½ part basil, unless, of course, you prefer more basil.

run, run, run, as fast as you can

My goose was cooked from the minute Inky's kindergarten teacher correctly pegged me as an artsy type with little capacity for saying no. No one else would do, she intimated, clutching my arm to prevent me from exiting with the rest of the herd. No other parent could bring such creative flair to the gingerbread-man station at the class party known in our culturally sensitive public school as a "pre-winter break celebration." Oh, she'd find projects for the mothers who actually *enjoyed* volunteering, remedial stuff like construction-paper crowns and glitter-glue pinecones, maybe they could help hand out juice or something. But decorating gingerbread men? That required skill and, I discovered shortly after saying yes, a presumed willingness to underwrite the entire operation.

In addition to footing the bill for enough frosting and sprinkles to satisfy the decorative impulses of twenty-three five-year-olds, I was expected to prebake the cookies the children would later personalize in my presence, their creative fires stoked by my shining aesthetic example.

"And when I say gingerbread, I mean, you know, sugar cookies," Teacher exclaimed, giddy now that she'd gotten what she wanted. "It's the shape, not the flavor." Right. Where had I heard that before?

Had I been a bit quicker on the draw, I could have wriggled out of this chore by alluding to painful memories I wished to avoid stirring up, some variant of *Gee, I wish I could chaperone that field trip, but ever since I saw my father getting eaten by that lion, I can't even walk past a zoo without crying.* The truth is, while most of my youthful experiences with pastry were positive, gingerbread men were always problematic.

Every Christmas, my mother was possessed by a mania to re-create the spirit of the season as it was celebrated in Colonial Williamsburg. Nowhere was this mandate more strictly enforced than in the realm of holiday baking. While other friends were having themselves a gay old time, glopping fluorescent icing and all manner of wang-dang-doodles onto tacky Santas and reindeer, I was carrying out Mistress Betsy's fanatical bidding as sheet after sheet of the molasses-flavored fuckers emerged from the oven. Maternal control freakery dictated that the ginger colonists' clothing was not to be slathered on, but merely indicated by narrow bands of white icing piped along coordinates consistent with hemlines and suspenders. No hair, though it was permissible to outfit the skirted girl figures with an optional head ornament consisting of a dab of green icing and a single Red Hot holly berry, Red Hots being the *The Williamsburg Cookbook*'s one concession to modernity. Currant eyes and Red Hot lips had been pressed into the dough before baking.

How could ingredients so magically capable of turning canned pears into baby bunnies assume such vapidity as the face of a human-shaped cookie? Their minimalism might have impressed the teachers and neighbors who received them by the plateload, but "decorating" them was about as joyous as stitching the soles onto Nikes so the family will have enough money to send big brother to school. If only I'd had a brother, we could have pelted each other with "holly berries" until Mom told us to get the hell out so she could clean up the goddamn mess in peace. Why do other families have all the fun?

Perhaps if I'd let Inky's teacher in on this youthful yuletide trauma, I could've scored myself a transfer to the no-advance-preparation-required potato-print table. Instead, there I was on the eve of the big shindig, trolling the aisles of Met Foods in a truly Grinchy frame of mind. It was a lucky break that the teacher considered traditional gingerbread men unappetizing to the childish palate, because if memory served, my mother's two-hundred-year-old recipe was a real bitch to whip up, requiring the purchase of all sorts of things I would likely never use again, like nutmeg and mace.

Not that Gran's sugar-cookie dough was a walk in the park, either. It dirtied a sink's worth of bowls and required chilling, as well as sifting. What a drag. Much as I love the picturesque old sifter I picked up at Amvets when equipping my college kitchen, I felt unwilling to invest that much energy on a kiddie project I'd done nothing to initiate. No doubt there are some New York City elementary schools where a child will find herself ostracized if her mother brings in the "wrong" kind of cookies, but thankfully, I can't afford their tuition. When it dawned on me that I could cut my prep time in half by eschewing flour and eggs for a few tubes of Pillsbury Ready to Bake dough, my path became clear. I like to think that Betty Crocker would have approved.

Ordinarily, I avoided this stuff. Spending time with Gran-Gran had warped me in such a way that I felt sorry for kids who associated baking not with stirring and rolling, but slicing. I might have been a know-nothing little k-pod in other ways, but goddamnit, I was serious about helping my grandmother cook, really getting in there and getting my hands dirty. That's not how the "dirty" sugar cookies we made together got their name, by the way. She called them "dirty" because my hands were so filthy to begin with.

Even so, she let me help. I got such a kick out of watching the dry ingredients absorb the wet and the process whereby things that tasted bad on their own, like flour, vanilla, and eggs, combined to become that ambrosial substance known as raw cookie dough. Fortunately, my grandmother wasn't the type to freak out about little things like salmonella or pinworms. She just let me do my thing. I loved dusting my pin and calculating where to place the cutters for the most efficient jigsaw fit, the one that would yield the most shamrocks, hearts, or turkeys per rolled-out sheet. When the scrap dough became too skimpy to accommodate a single cutter, Gran would use an overturned juice glass to press out a final circle, or sometimes let me keep the surplus so I could continue to pretend that I was in charge.

My only significant interaction with Pillsbury Ready to Bake came when my dorm mates and I, seeking to combat some powerful munchies, nuked it in microwave-proof cereal bowls. The resultant tongue-searing sludge had served its purpose, but otherwise, I'd always considered this product vastly inferior to the homemade model it purports to replicate. On the other hand, there are no atheists in foxholes, and hadn't the teacher herself declared that flavor mattered not a jot when compared to shape?

The problem began when I got home and attempted to roll out my prefabricated dough. Actually, the problem might have started on the walk home, when, skidding on a patch of ice, there was this moment where I believed that my groceries were worth more than my body. Didn't bruise so much as a pear, but the resulting back pain was such that even thc simple act of making room in the refrigerator for a quart of milk and a dozen (unbroken) eggs brought me close to tears. The only way I could roll out the dough was to kneel on the floor before the counter, the pin held level with my ears, all the while whimpering, "It hurts. It hurts."

"Are you sure you want to go through with this?" Greg asked, peering at this pathetic spectacle from the safety of the doorway.

"What's the alternative?" I snapped, with the fatalistic resolve of a furry creature preparing to chew its foot free of a trap.

"I don't know. Maybe something from that bakery on Court Street . ?"

"No bakery sells undecorated sugar cookies shaped like gingerbread men!" I hissed as my aching back spasmed anew. Fortunately, somewhere in that all-enveloping cloak of pain, there was a tiny pinprick of light, a reminder not to squander energy on such inessentials as tearing my solution-seeking husband a new A-hole. "You know what you could do for me? Occupy the children. I can do this, but not if they're in here trying to 'help.'" They hadn't yet ventured in, but I knew them well enough to know it was only a matter of time.

"Are you sure? I'll bet if you just called the school and explained—"

"Who's going to answer the phone after hours?" I spat. "Go watch the children."

"What's Mommy doing?" I could hear Inky asking as Greg rounded them up.

"Mama!" Milo keened. "Mama!" There was a burst of footsteps as he was apprehended midflight and dragged into the bedroom, howling.

"Who wants a puppet show?" Greg cried in one of the high-pitched character voices that the children love so well. Milo wailed. Fa la la la la, la la la la! God bless us every one!

"Don't let them in here!" I reiterated, hobbling forward with a wooden spoon, just in case.

Why not lie down and deputize Greg to make the damn cookies? Well, for one thing, his repertoire at the time was limited to spaghetti and eggs, and for the other, let's just say that maternal control freakery doesn't fall far from the culinary tree. Making homemade eggnog every New Year's wreaked havoc on my mother's mental equilibrium, but I recognized that the situation would have deteriorated further had my noncooking stepfather offered to take over. (He must have, too, since he never did.) The pink-cheeked guests calling tidings of comfort and joy from the threshold expected the quality their hostess, even at the peak of her annual nervous breakdown, was hell-bent to deliver, not the feeble attempts of some well-meaning but ineffectual sub. Had Inky's teacher not singled me out as the only parent equal to this task? I would come through if it killed me. Grunting in pain, I wielded the secondhand wooden pin that dated, like the sifter, to my undergraduate days, when I believed homegrown piecrusts were an indispensable component of the earth-mamahood to which I aspired. How could that idealistic young girl have anticipated the miserable circumstances of this, the first situation in years to require its use?

Alarmingly, the rolling pin turned out to be an imposition that the dough seemed to resent. Despite liberal preflouring, the wooden shaft soon became coated with a petroleum-like substance and the dough semitransparent, in the way of a paper sack absorbing french fry grease. It occurred to me that Poppin' Fresh might have put some heavy-duty preservatives in this shit before packing it into its tubes, compounds that could be sliced to no ill effect, but reacted in bizarre and hideous ways to the friction of the rolling pin. Despite mounting hysteria, I pressed on, praying the three ibuprofen I had swallowed, along with six hundred or so calories' worth of raw dough, would start to kick in.

I think it was Goethe who said something like, "Happiness recalled in times of sadness is the saddest thing of all." Picturing Gran's and my dirty sugar cookies made me want to lie down on the floor and sob. Our unbaked cookie shapes transferred from wax paper rolling surface to metal baking sheet so obediently, I had performed this task while in nursery school. By contrast, the unwholesome product with which I was now working clung to the Formica on which it had been rolled with the tenacity of a mollusk. I would have had to major in surgery to separate the fragile tissues of the kindergartners' gingerbread men from the matrix of my kitchen counter. My spatula threatened to wipe out the entire population. The way they were rucking back upon themselves reminded me of an attempt at age eight to dry-shave my legs, an experiment that predictably caused an inchlong strip of skin to pleat up like Venetian blinds.

Every once in a while, I'd manage to get one of the little bastards clear of the counter, only to have its wimpy limbs drop off en route to the tray. The overworked dough had long ago lost its chill, but I couldn't bear the thought of prolonging the agony by returning it to the fridge for the hour it would take to cool back down to the recommended temperature. The radiant pain still plaguing my lower back was not helping matters, either. After a couple of attempts to reclaim the situation by throwing out the whole mess and starting afresh, there was real danger that I'd run out of dough. I'd been at it an hour and had exactly one cookie lined up on the sheet. It was missing a part of its head.

"How are things going in there?" Greg called from the children's bedroom. "Do you think you'll be done soon?"

"Just keep out until I tell you!"

I cursed as yet another flaccid limb fell off, too oily and overwrought to maintain structural integrity. Christ, they were rotten to the core, like the stems of cut flowers left moldering for weeks in water unchanged since they were first put in a vase. Pure slime.

Would it upset a five-year-old to decorate a double amputee? How about a headless corpse? At the rate the cookies were decapitating themselves, maybe we'd be better off stringing popcorn or something, not that I had enough needles to go around, or even popcorn.

I could no longer stand. Could this have been what it was like for the little old hunchback lady who used to sit at the lunch counter of the Sherman Snack Shop, drinking her coffee with a straw, her nose just centimeters away from the scrambled eggs Ed the busboy cut into manageable pieces for her? She was always so cheerful. I couldn't imagine smiling. Ever again.

I dragged another tube of dough from the fridge, sliced it into rounds on the kitchen floor, admitted defeat. We'd just have to decorate circles. Stupid, Pillsbury Ready to Bake circles that a potato-print mom could have spearheaded instead of me. I glowered at the polka dots lined up on my baking tray, wishing I could chuck the entire batch out our third-story kitchen window. Stupid, stupid, stupid. *Wait.* Suddenly, inspiration struck. One circle could be the head. One circle could be the body. Another circle could be matchsticked and turned into limbs. . . .

Raw, they had a sort of Venus of Willendorf–y charm. Baked, they could have passed for starfish, but, determined to see this thing through, I mocked up a sample using Apple Jacks for eyes and cross-sectioning a red gumdrop for a maw as gaping and lurid as an inflatable sex doll's. Colonial Williamsburg would have been scandalized. I loved it more than words can say.

Fortunately, the teacher didn't take the least bit of umbrage at my gingerbread men's anarchic shape. Perhaps she considered this just more evidence of my golden creativity. The guests of honor didn't give a shit, either, particularly the little psycho who kept dipping his tongue in and out of a plastic tub of rainbow sprinkles, his eyes rolling like an unbroken pony's. They passed through my station in groups of five, gunking up their cookies with neon-hued frostings cobbled together from food coloring and the confectioners' sugar I'd limped out to buy from the all-night bodega at 11:00 PM the previous night, to the tune of $4.99 a box. When the young decorators wanted to switch colors, they simply licked their plastic knives and dug right in.

Too fried to offer much in the way of artistic guidance, or even adult supervision, I smiled benignly up from the floor. They dumped fistfuls of red and green sugar on everything within a five-foot radius. Fine with me. No one had the slightest interest in the raisins my upbringing had compelled me to schlep along, though the Apple Jacks went fast. The whole scene was vaguely reminiscent of Karen Finley's early work.

"Inky's Mom! Inky's Mom! Raheem's eating his!" one of the little girls shrieked as her neighbor chomped down on a starfish-shaped slab fortified with flaked, sweetened coconut an inch thick. I shrugged noncommittally, glad that somebody thought these turkeys were edible.

"But he's not supposed to!" the tattler insisted, outraged by what she took to be indifference on my part. "They not for eating! They for show!"

"You may be right there," I agreed pleasantly. "Half-right, anyway."

The teacher swung by to compliment me on coming through (unlike a certain no-show potato-print volunteer). I wasn't entirely satisfied that she appreciated the emotional and physical hurdles I'd surmounted in order to hold up my end of the bargain, but etiquette compelled me to winch myself into a semiseated position in order to apologize for my baked goods' untraditional shape.

Waving a hand mottled with glitter, dried Elmer's, red and green tempera, and a few shreds of coconut, Teacher lowered her voice to reassure me that the kids didn't know the difference. "As long as it tastes good!" she chuckled, tacking off toward another stooge's pinecone staging area. I lay back down. Having verified that Teacher was no longer concerned with gingerbread, three children set to avidly licking the table.

dirty sugar cookies

Preheat the oven to 350°, except not yet because the dough's going to have to chill for at least an hour.

Put your sifter (amazing how much use you get out of that thing) onto a salad plate, then pour in:

3 cups of flour
1 teaspoon of baking powder
¼ teaspoon of salt
1¼ cup of sugar

Position the sifter over a big mixing bowl, lose the salad plate, and crank away.

Alternatively, you may chuck your dry ingredients directly into the mixing bowl and give them a couple of twirls with a meat fork.

Add 1 cup of shortening (or 2 sticks of butter if you're some sort of health nut).

Next, crack 3 eggs directly into the bowl. Do not beat them first. This is how my grandmother did it, and quite possibly how they did it in Colonial Williamsburg as well.

Then add 1 teaspoon of vanilla. Knock yourself out with the aforementioned meat fork.

Cover the dough with plastic wrap and put it in the fridge. If you want to pretend it's Pillsbury Ready to Bake, you can roll it into a cylinder before you wrap it up.

At some point, cover your work surface with wax paper. Sprinkle some flour on both the wax paper and your rolling pin. Roll out the dough. Dip the cookie cutters in some flour. Line the unbaked cookies up on a metal baking sheet. Preheat the oven you forgot to preheat earlier. If you want to go for the minimalist raisin-eye look, now's the time to press them into the dough. You can also festoon them with colored sugars.

Bake each batch for 8 to 10 minutes, then cool. Transfer carefully so as to avoid limb loss.

Ice as you dare.

acorn vs. the tree

Somewhere in Indiana, my mother is savoring this turn of events: In a stunning example of divine payback, the universe has dealt me a picky eater.

Speaking as a former finicky eight-year-old, I wish I could be more empathetic, but for some reason her retarded palate drives me totally fucking batshit. I can't take her to Chinatown! I mean, I do, she loves it there, but the only things she'll eat are coconut buns and white rice. The waiters must think I'm starving an innocent child. Maybe they see her as just another spoiled American brat dissing their motherland's proud cuisine. Either way, it looks bad.

"Inky, how can I take you to Japan or India when you refuse to eat perfectly delicious dumplings just five subway stops from home?"

"You're not eating them," she points out.

"Only because I'm a vegetarian."

"You eat fish."

"Yeah, well, that's another thing I wish you'd eat. Come on, take a bite." If she doesn't get some food in her soon, both of us are in danger of becoming hypoglycemic, which is to say bitchy, at least in my case.

"I tried these before," she bleats, panicking as I blow on a dumpling to cool it for her sampling pleasure. Little fabulist. Who cares how many lips and anuses this plump parcel contains? It smells divine. I'd eat it myself if I weren't so damn tenderhearted.

"You've never tried these before," I correct her, as single-minded as that android guy who keeps coming after Arnold Schwarzenegger in *Terminator 2*, unfazed by bullets and impalement. The dumpling bumps against her tightly sealed lips. "You're going to love it." Her eyes roll, desperately seeking a possible escape route, but there is none. "You're lucky. Mommy didn't have Chinatown growing up." Her neck strains as she squinches her mouth away from dumpling invader, or maybe she's just repulsed by the ick factor of me referring to myself in the third person, the way I did when she was in diapers.

"You're being ridiculous," I chide, all sorts of promises I once made to myself regarding the upbringing of my then-unborn children beginning to shear away like so much failed airplane cable. She looks stricken, she looks just like I looked at eight, but there's no stuffing Bitchmother back in her hole this late in the game.

"All right," I give in, with a self-pitying sigh so hateful, any drag queen happening by would canonize me on the spot. "I'll let you off the hook this time. But no dessert, and," I pause dramatically, "you have to take a courtesy bite." Jesus, what kind of monster am I? She might want to start hiding the wire hangers.

*

The only positive thing that can be said for Inky's chow-time reticence is that it's saved me from falling into one of maternity's most pernicious traps. I admit to having dressed my baby in attention-getting hipster duds. I have angered the childless by repeating adorable utterances and toting her to adults-only events. But I have never, ever disgraced myself by boasting about what a good eater I have. And believe me, given the opportunity, I'm sure I would have.

I entered this racket full of blind faith that a well-intentioned mother can mold a child's appetite, provided she starts early enough and consults a child-rearing manual different from the one my mother must have used in 1965. I planned to get a jump on things by reading up on this and other subjects in a left-of-mainstream parenting magazine a shower-attending friend had subscribed to on my behalf. I passed untold hours of nesting time reviewing ads for all-natural cleaning supplies, cotton diapers and goddess-worshipping baby slings. As far as fantasy views of the near future go, this rag rivaled *Seventeen*. Luscious-looking pregnant women with long, red ringlets labored nude in candlelit hot tubs, surrounded by supportive friends and family. Appealing toddlers in unbleached cotton garb occupied themselves with wooden toys. There were even picnics! Hoo, boy, I couldn't wait to get that bun out of the oven in order to join their ranks.

Having swallowed this rosy vision hook, line, and sinker, it was jarring to open a new issue and find it all abristle with angry letters to the editor. Usually, readers' comments stayed well within the realm of the positive, thanking the staff for providing such a loving, nonjudgmental forum and inquiring where readers could buy the gorgeous handknit booties the model was wearing in a recent feature about cosleeping in Nepal. Surprisingly, the article that elicited this firestorm of scorching feedback was not some uppity opinion piece about the decision to vaccinate or wean, but a seemingly good-humored how-to on getting children to eat healthfully, written from a first-person perspective. I remembered it well, because I'd happily placed all my eggs in that author's basket. This time next year, I too would know the joy of feeding an enthusiastic little chick, all apeep for more of Mama's wholesome home cooking. Yep, there's a sucker born every minute, but judging from their letters, plenty of subscribers weren't hoodwinked in the least.

"Self-congratulatory claptrap," sniped one.

"Isn't it wonderful that the author's sixteen-month-old daughter adores veal piccata," another seethed. "How about some real advice for those of us whose offspring are merely average?"

While relishing this bitchfest from the sidelines, I still managed to consider myself above the fray. First off, veal piccata was a moot point with me. I might not have given birth yet, but if I knew anything, it was that no child of mine would soil his or her perfect temple with the flesh of another helpless baby, particularly one who'd spent the entirety of its miserable life in a lightless crate. Furthermore, following a lengthy period in which mother's milk would provide the sole source of nourishment, my child was going to eat everything I offered without coaxing or complaint: spinach, quinoa, carrot juice, Penang curry, shrimp roti, French onion soup, vegetarian dumplings in Chinatown . . . oh ha ha ha ha ha. Is it too late to write a letter to the editor?

*

Unlike his sister, my five-year-old, Milo, is what you'd call a "good eater." (I mean, I wouldn't, but only because I'm now on record as never having disgraced myself with that specific snippet of self-congratulation, so vexing to those of us who must daily wrangle with a good eater's opposite.) The boy's table manners could use some improvement, but as long as the grub goes down the gullet, I'm cool with tossing chunks of his dinner under the table, so he can pretend he's a caged lion tearing into hunks of zebra and antelope. Under duress, and depending on the condition of the floor, I've occasionally let this charade transpire in restaurants. Of course, even when he deigns to remain in his chair, he knows how to play us.

"Do that again, Daddy!" he shrieks, withholding his next mouthful until Greg hoots across the neck of his empty beer bottle like a one-man oompah band. "Mommy, make that farting noise! Tell that story about the elephant! More chocolate milk!" On home turf, we cave in to many of these demands, knowing that he'll make good on his end, eventually cleaning his plate of roasted cauliflower, ginger-steamed tilapia, or some other nutritious, home-cooked delicacy currently causing his sister to wilt like three-week-old bok choy.

"Inky, eat!" Greg thunders, coming to the end of his tether midway through the meal. "Your mother went to the trouble of cooking this delicious meal for us!" (Yeah, like that'll convince her. She saw me leaning on the kitchen counter, idly perusing the latest *Eating Well* when I was supposed to be putting water on for the mac and cheese I'd promised to make her if she cleaned her room, did her homework, and stayed out of my hair while I spent two hours checking email.) "Look at your baby brother! He's eating his!"

Just for the record, Mommy and Daddy both consider it a mistake to cast the kids as some sort of culinary Cain and Abel, but it sure is tempting when the one chews her courtesy bite to a gag-inducing paste unfit for swallowing and the other inhales extra helpings of raw baby spinach, pausing only to belt out a quick chorus of "Popeye the Sailor Man."

Well-intentioned friends and family have suggested that involving Inky in food preparation might expand her palate. Like I hadn't thought of that, despite the steadfastness with which I balked at eating the cottage cheese tails I'd so lovingly deposited on the hind ends of Betty Crocker's canned-pear bunnies. As long as it has chocolate chips in it, she's willing to go the distance, but everything else has proved a bust, if consumption was the ultimate goal. The fallout of this experiment is that now she *loves* to cook. In this respect, she's the child I'd always dreamed of having.

Unfortunately, it's just one more department in which I'm not quite shaping up to be the mother I'd figured myself for. It seems I'm not so much a delightful hybrid of Laura Ingalls' Ma and the cast of *Zoom* as a stressed-out dandelion wishing someone would pop her damn head off already. An eggshell shattering into a bowlful of batter can take five minutes off my life. It hardly matters that it's been months since the kitchen floor was mopped when every spill makes me feel like I'm on the verge of an aneurysm.

"You're holding the grater the wrong way again!" I bark. "Oh my god, look at your filthy subway paws!" I can't remember any of my female relatives displaying this level of intolerance, though to be fair, I never knew Gran as the mother of small children and Mom had but one would-be chef to contend with, in addition to the option of sending me around the corner to Grandma's whenever the going got hairy.

Maybe it would be different if we were just cooking for cooking's sake, but always on my end, there's this tiny flicker of hope that this time, the con will work. Such optimism, however meager, is folly when the mark is a child who hates lasagna. As do I. All the more reason to get royally pissed when I wind up having to eat it three nights in a row, lest it go to waste. Believe me, if I could send it to the Sudan, I would.

It's so unfair," Inky wails as, across from her, her younger brother, unbothered, dispatches his allotted portion of an entrée she cannot bring herself to taste. Twenty minutes into yet another indescribably jolly family meal, this outburst manages to penetrate the permafrost surrounding my inflexible adult heart, just a bit. Seems like only yesterday that I was the powerless child facing a plate full of insurmountable courtesy bites. I didn't *want* to be a bad eater. Was it my fault that the kinds of food I liked weren't traditional dinnertime fare? If Pop-Tarts, powdered Jell-O, and Count Chocula could have replaced meat loaf, salad, and stewed tomatoes, I'd have packed it away like Paul Bunyan.

The nightly battle over Inky's pitiful intake would cease if only the chef could bring herself to whittle the menu to just two surefire items, black beans and Annie's Mac & Cheese prepared à la Greg, who makes me look bad by taking that extra step, dumping the noodles into a colander so the pot is free for him to create a roux of butter and powdered cheese. Yes, no doubt, Inky would get behind this approach. To use her father's term, she doesn't give a hell that the mere mention of black beans sends Milo into a major fucking hissy fit. Makes me long for the days when all a mommy had to do to earn herself a nice long rest at the sanitarium was run screaming into the street with her hair uncombed, wearing something that looked like a nightie. Shit, I do that all the time.

"Honey, you're getting yourself worked up over nothing," I console the girl with unexpected, if rote, kindness, brought on by fatigue or something like it. I can feel my stake in the outcome ebbing away, as if I'm hovering just under the ceiling, a disembodied spectator to the trauma in which we are embroiled below. Suddenly suffering the slings and arrows of outrageous fortune sounds like a lot less hassle than taking arms and by opposing . . . whatever it was that Hamlet said. Why force the kid to eat if she doesn't want to? Let her coast by with a vitamin, or better yet, from here on out, let's just dump a couple of packs of Lunchables in front of the tube and call that dinner, because I'm sick of browbeating an innocent child like a Hogarth in hipster's clothing.

"You know," I say, assuming a confidential, just-us-girls tone, now that Greg has stalked off to load the dishwasher and Milo is flaunting the privileges of the Clean Plate Club by lollygagging on the rug with a toy catalog the two of them nearly killed each other over earlier, "I used to be a picky eater, too—"

"Stop calling me that," she howls, punching her placemat in frustration.

Okay . . . "Want to know what I think, sweetie?" I press, struggling not to let my Glinda the Good veer into Margaret Hamilton. "You're tired after a long day at school, and what you need more than anything is fuel so your body can run and play and do all the fun things it likes to do. Remember what Daddy told you about cars needing gas?"

"I'm not tired!" she yells.

That makes one of us. She looks like I feel, a couple of heartbeats shy of total, screaming meltdown. "Look, Inky," I say, the magic bubble in which the Good Witch floated unceremoniously and irrevocably popped, "I'll make black beans tomorrow, but tonight, you're just going to have to bite the bullet and eat some fish. Because that's what we're having. *Comprende?*" Her shoulders ride up past her ears, and I understand that as much as she wants to, she just can't. Though maybe with a bit of maternal encouragement . . . "I'll . . . I'll . . . let you do your Easy-Bake Oven tomorrow."

Oh my god, I can't tell whether I'm desperate or just plain demented. It's madness to breach the out of sight, out of mind policy I put into place by stashing the lightbulb-powered faux microwave she received for her sixth birthday in the leakiest recesses of our below-sink kitchen cabinet, behind some paint cans and an assortment of household poisons. I'm resigned that every so often she'll remember she owns the infernal thing and drag it out, but never have I voluntarily suggested its use. Upholding the fine tradition my own mother started by declining to buy any mix beyond that which came packaged with my toy oven ultimately creates more problems than it solves. Several times a year, my reserves of flour and sugar must be exposed to the eager gropings of a less-than-exacting Easy Baker (and her grubby apprentice).

Having given the project my extremely conflicted blessing when resorting to it as my best-odds dinnertime bribe, I am now obliged to stay out of range, for the truest reward of this "toy" is the illusion that one is fending for oneself. The only thing worse than having some bitchy adult hovering over your shoulder, issuing unwanted proclamations in regard to sharing, precise measurements, and slowing down is being that bitchy adult. I'll have plenty of time to explore that role once the kids have moved on to some other activity, leaving me to survey a mess whose cleanup will most certainly exceed the ten minutes the forgotten cowpat must spend under its 120-watt bulb. Lucky for Inky, she chronically forgets to grease her pan before slopping in the batter. Her pucklike pastry's refusal to come out in one clean piece short-circuits my wrath, plunging me back into the stormy seas of childhood's myriad disappointments, an experience that's all the more wrenching for being vicarious. If I only had a penny, or better yet a shot of mescal, for every ambition thwarted, for all the things that don't turn out right.

Thoroughly chastened, I divide the crumbly mess between four saucers and serve it after a less-taxing-than-usual family meal, oohing and ahhing like one unaccustomed to such rich splendors. Greg is on the same page, willing to postpone the pint of Cherry Garcia in the freezer until the kids are in bed, out of respect for the chef. The chef, however, has other ideas. To Inky's way of thinking, this ship docked when she slid the pan into the oven, using the very same footlong, pronged purple plastic pushing implement professional bakers use to avoid burning themselves. No need to stick around for the dreary denouement.

"Is it okay with you if maybe we have something else?" she asks, her desire for a decent dessert edging out her anxiety over disappointing the covetous parents whose happiness hinges on this baking powder–less treat, as much as Grampy's once did on a Laughner's child's plate. "Or you can have it all," she offers, with a bright duplicity all too humiliatingly recognizable as a dead ringer for my own.

"Maybe we should save it," I propose.

"In case you change your mind and want some later," Greg adds.

"Or you want some later," Inky replies, before Milo saves us all by falling asleep right at the table without having changed into pajamas, brushed his teeth, or, more problematically, voided his bladder. Even if this turn of events ends in a wet bed, it's also a welcome excuse to bring the face-saving to a satisfying conclusion. We wouldn't dream of excluding little brother from sampling a goody he helped create. To proceed without Milo would be wrong. Especially since by morning, he's likely to have forgotten that nasty cake ever existed.

As Greg excuses himself to scoop ice cream into three chipped teacups, I gather the four portions of untouched crumbs, positioning them waitress style along my forearm.

"You know, I almost took you up on your offer to split it with Daddy, but then I figured maybe it's nicer if we all eat the same thing. What do you think?" With ice cream on its way and the maddeningly good eater down for the count, it's hardly surprising that this time, we find ourselves in complete agreement.

inky's sesame–fried tofu with brown rice and broccoli

I once served this recipe to a kid who thought everything but white bread was gross . . . and not only did she not burst into tears, she asked for seconds and said I was a better cook than her mother . . . in front of her mother.

Make a pot of brown rice. If you require instructions, do an Internet search or join a commune.

Chop a couple of heads of broccoli, and if you're not too picky, peel and slice the stalks.

Drain a 14-oz container of firm tofu, blot it dry, and chop it into cubes.

Chop 3 to 6 cloves of garlic.

Fire up your big heavy skillet over a medium flame, add a child-sized handful of sesame seeds, and stir constantly. Don't turn your back because the second you do, they'll turn into cremains, and nobody wants to eat those.

Lower the heat, add 3 tablespoons of olive oil and your chopped garlic, which requires the same vigilance you showed its friends, the sesame seeds. You're going for toasted marshmallow brown, not accidentally stuck-it-in-the-fire black.

Now crank the heat to high, throw in the tofu, stir it a bit so it's coated with garlic and sesame, and then quit hovering! It's not a baby! God! Just turn it every couple of minutes with a spatula to tan all sides of the cubes. Don't fret if some outer layers weld to the pan. Them's just vegetarian cracklin's, son!

When the tofu's browned, sprinkle with 1 tablespoon of sesame oil, 3 tablespoons of soy sauce,* and 1/4 cup of water.

Chuck in the broccoli, stir to coat, cover the pan, and let it steam for five minutes or so. (You can save this step for later if the brown rice is far from done. Plan to resume operations a few minutes before dinner.)

Serve atop brown rice, and don't turn into Bitchmother just because you have to wash your stovetop. Like it wasn't all spattered up before. . . .

**Note: Purchasing my family's clothes at the Salvation Army allows me to drive the Cadillac of soy sauces, Dashi Soy, from Kamada Foods. Search the Web, and soon they'll be mailing you cunning little milk cartons of luxury-priced soy sauce brewed the way the shoguns liked it!*

a different kind of chicken

A few years ago, my mother summoned me back to Indianapolis. My grandfather was moving into a retirement community, and I could no longer put off dealing with the twenty-one boxes Greg and I had stashed in his "spare room" when we moved from Chicago to New York. Sorting through reams of memorabilia usually holds all the juicy appeal of leafing through old yearbooks drunk, but the movers' imminent arrival afforded me little time to dilly-dally. To complicate matters further, I'd had no choice but to drag three-year-old Inky and the infant Milo along for the ride. This didn't leave me feeling particularly charitable toward their father when I started slitting open boxes to discover that five years earlier, Greg had packed by upending his desk drawers directly into the cartons I dragged home for him from the grocery and liquor stores. My task would drag on far beyond my initial estimate thanks to his damn greeting cards, out-of-date résumés, foreign coins, and I don't know what all.

My mother, grossly aggrieved to see me falling behind schedule, suggested chucking the whole lot, but I couldn't in good conscience do that when I'd just unearthed Greg's only photographs of his late father, sandwiched between two old utility bills. Grampy kept getting into boxes my mother had sealed up for the movers, Milo howled to nurse, and Mom seemed to be letting the tension get to her in a way it hadn't since the great Heart-Shaped Waffle Incident of February '83.

Not the most conducive atmosphere for saying a proper goodbye to the house my grandparents had lived in since I was eight, the closest thing I had to a house in which I grew up. How many hours had I spent sprawled on the family room's braided rag rug, eating peppermint ice cream and drinking Gran's homemade milkshakes while waiting for something better than *Hee Haw* to come on? Every day after school, there was a plate of cheese cubes, Ritz crackers, and sliced summer sausage waiting for me, as well as a small glass packed vertically with salted carrot sticks.

In summer, I idled in the shade of the carport, choking back bitter iced tea in order to reach the delightful sugar sediment at the bottom of the glass. Then, after Gran snagged a red plaid hammock at a garage sale, I took to repairing to the side yard with a dozen or so chocolate chip cookies, to spy on Mr. Doyle mowing his lawn next door. Time had always seemed to pass so slowly in this house, and now I didn't have enough of it. To add insult to injury, the between-meal snacks that had once marked the hours as reliably as clock chimes had dried up so completely that my mother had had to drive to Pizza Hut when Inky started whining from hunger.

I might have grown up here, but now little was left to tether me to the surroundings. The shelves had been stripped of their customary curios. The hammock was gone, like, really gone, not just bundled into the toolshed for the winter. When Greg and I dropped off our boxes en route to New York, the "spare room" had still been recognizable as Gran's bedroom. Now it was as impersonal as the stripped mattress dominating it. Apparently, Grampy had swept through, appropriating everything that wasn't nailed down to donate to his church's rummage sale. That's where the hammock had gone, and the aluminum iced-tea glasses that would have fetched a fortune on eBay. "Yessir, they're going to have to change the name from Second Presbyterian to Saint Robert's!" he announced more than once, displaying all the sentiment of a toucan.

In addition to Greg's and my stuff, I had a mental list of Gran's belongings that I hoped to bring back to New York. They were of little monetary value, and decidedly impractical for a New York City apartment-dweller making do with but one closet (for a family of four), but the heart wants what it wants. Many of the tokens I sought to claim, like the hammock and the frumpy flowered Easter chapeaux Gran stored in glamorous round hatboxes, were nowhere to be found. Some she might even have thrown away herself. I didn't really expect there'd be much chance of finding the small scrap of paper she used to carry in her billfold, on which, at the tender age of three, I'd drawn a portrait of the two of us. I'd captured her with her bosom stuck out farther than a cow-catcher, and I located myself somewhere to its starboard, hovering like a creepy little saucer-eyed alien.

"Oh no, I haven't the foggiest what would have happened to that," my mother told me. "Do you want the good silver?"

No, I wanted the family film reels. Unfortunately, according to my mother, Grampy had burned them.

"Burned them?" I cried. Surely this was incorrect. Giving Gran's old cloth coats to the church was one thing. Deliberately torching home movies of Cousin Lou Ann and me skipping in circles and waving the day she graduated from high school was quite another. What on earth could have driven my whistling, change-jingling grandfather to such a malevolent, melodramatic, and above all, permanent act?

"Ayun, I have no idea," my mother sighed.

And then, go figure, the films turned up safe and sound on a shelf recently vacated by the guest towels, downgrading the mystery from why Grampy would behave like Mr. Rochester to why, this late in the game, an old man still possessed of his mental faculties would bother relocating a dusty and fairly heavy box of inessentials from one closet to another.

More than anything, I longed to walk with Gran's recipe box. Not wanting to seem presumptuous, I offered Gran's only daughter first dibs on this treasure, but Mom immediately demurred.

"Are you sure?" I pressed, hoping she wasn't subjugating her desires so that I might realize mine.

"Ayun, please. I think it's sweet that you want it. It would have made Gran very happy."

Except we couldn't find it. So help me if my arsonist grandfather had used it to kindle his Duraflame! Part of the problem might have been that Mom was busy looking for a metal index-card file I had collaged in third grade when the recipe box I recalled was white wood with a chicken painted on it.

"I could have sworn you made a recipe box with your class one year," she said midway through the search. "Don't you remember? It had little dollhouse food glued to the top of it."

"Yes, but Mom, I gave that to you."

"Oh," she said vaguely, "I think you're right." She returned her attention to Inky's coloring book with suspicious swiftness, while I went to pay yet another call on the open cabinet by the kitchen window, hoping that the recipe box had rematerialized in the five minutes since I'd last looked. No, the cabinet was still empty, but I'd eaten so many lunches across from it, I could have plotted its former contents in my sleep. All those propped-up commemorative Christmas plates. We'd given Gran one a year for as far back as I could remember. A black metal trivet shaped like a spade. A rustic figurine we had brought back for her when we visited Missy in Tucson, depicting a robed, friarish person the gift shop lady had identified as the patron saint of cooking. And on the second shelf, or maybe the one right above it, Gran's wooden recipe box. "Are you sure you don't remember moving it?" I badgered my mother. No, all she remembered was taking the Christmas plates.

And then, just as I was pushing off Greg's and my last box, she made a big deal about entering the spare room on tiptoe, towing Inky along behind her. "Tell Mommy what we found," she coached.

I didn't need to be told. "Where was it?" I screamed.

"Hiding in plain sight on that little shelf behind the can opener. You know, next to the sink. As soon as I saw it, everything fell into place. That's where she always kept it, Ayun, not that cabinet you kept talking about."

Hmm. Grampy had mentioned something about his new retirement community having an Alzheimer's wing. Maybe given this business with the recipe box, they'd consider letting me move in there. Not that I haven't always had a mind like a perforated steel trap.

"Listen to this," I chuckled from the passenger's seat as we finally drove away from the house on Englewood Road. If Gran had been alive, she'd have been out under the carport or pressed up against the window, and Mom would have reminded me to wave. "Carolyn Bigler's Sauerkraut Salad. Lime Jell-O and 7-Up Salad. Noda's Raw Cranberry Salad—oh, right, their neighbor on Kenwood. I'd forgotten all about her. Whoo, her Cranberry Salad sounds gross." My mother flipped the turn signal without comment. Dealing with my grandfather and her grandchildren had wiped her out. Strangely, I felt energized, the way I do after a particularly triumphant thrift store score.

"Okay, here we go! God, just look at all these desserts. They take up half the box. Way to go, Gran! Chocolate Jumbos. Kentucky Derby Pie. Wait, what's this? Durbin Sugar Cream Pie: 1 cup sugar, 1/4 cup corn starch, 1 stick margarine—"

"Put it away," Mom cut me off, in a strangled-sounding voice. She swiped at her eyes with the heel of her hand. "I can't bear to look at it." This was highly irregular. I mist up at everything from school assemblies to *Morning Edition*, but the one who bore me is usually made of sterner stuff. The vacuum seal on her Ball jar is kept pretty tight. Sometimes, though, the lid is no match for the pressure of the contents.

I realized then that I was totally ignorant as to the history of Gran's red and white wooden box, painted, incidentally, with a rooster, not the chicken I recalled. Given that my mother was operating a motor vehicle under what, for her, was extreme emotional duress, the present moment didn't seem a particularly opportune time to start delving.

Maybe, like the musty sheet music and children's books I had rescued from Grampy's rummage sale pile, the recipe box predated me. Maybe my uncle Bill, a trucker whom we sort of lost touch with when he and his family moved to Florida, had made it for Gran in Boy Scouts. I flipped it over. JAPAN, stated a small sticker affixed to the bottom. Okay, so maybe he'd brought it back from the Air Force, like the beautiful silk kimono Gran once pulled from a bottom drawer to show me.

Right after the funeral, when Mom asked me if I wanted anything special as a keepsake of my grandmother, vintage clothes whore that I am, I asked for the kimono. It about blew my mind when Mom informed me that Gran had asked to be buried with it. (As opposed to in it, which would really have knocked me for a loop.) Had my stolid Hoosier grandmother, who loved Lawrence Welk and disapproved of me living with boys, gone to her grave harboring some lifelong secret desire to visit Kyoto? Or to be a geisha or something? What else didn't I know?

I had figured Gran's recipe box for some sort of reliquary, the holy vessel in which I would find the key to her mashed potatoes, her green beans, and her fried chicken. I know, I don't eat fried chicken, but it's an heirloom I'd have liked to be able to hand down to the kids. Most of the photographs that showed her as I remembered her were in albums that got packed away when my parents split up. Her speech was peppered with a number of distinctive, old-timey expressions, but try as I might, I'm no good at mimicking her uniquely grating, countrified voice. I could exclaim, "Well, for criminette!" till the cows come home and never succeed in bringing her to life for Greg and the kids. Not to my satisfaction, anyway. Her recipes struck me as the most concrete representation I would likely lay hold to, which is why I had been so intent on getting that box. It came jam-packed with recipe cards, all right. I just never would have anticipated that the ones I was after weren't in there.

The missing dishes were straightforward, old-fashioned fare, the kind of standards food editors like to jazz up with crème fraîche and infused vinegars before marketing them as exciting new spins on holiday classics. Although *Good Housekeeping* and *Ladies' Home Journal* were prominently displayed in her home, Gran spent her entire life reproducing the food she'd grown up eating. She probably absorbed the bulk of her signature recipes at her mother's knee, long before Baby Zibah, the last of her six brothers and sisters, was born. With that many kids, I doubt Great-Grandmother had had much time to fool with fancy ingredients, precise measurements, or even writing things down.

Actually, I did find one yellowing card designated, in Gran's unmistakable hand, as "Mother's Receipt." It was for sugar cookies, the "dirty" ones I'd always thought of as hers, and mine. For every hundred cookbooks published, there are probably eighty approximations of this recipe, but given the penmanship, it's an awfully nice souvenir, far more meaningful to me than those computer-generated family trees Grampy takes such pleasure in spitting out on the recently purchased PC he's christened Emily.

Few of the other recipes in the box rung a bell. Corned Beef Salad Mold? Mercedes Harris's Champagne Dessert? Given the ladies' luncheon feel of the titles, I could only conclude that bridge-club etiquette compelled her to ask for the recipe for every dish ever brought to a potluck. Even the ones attributed to my great-aunts weren't the sorts of things you'd feed a hungry farmhand. What shocked me about Gran's sisters' recipes was how credit had been assigned with surnames as well as first names. Was this really necessary? I'll grant you that Gran counted more than one Ruth among her acquaintances, but the odds of knowing two people named Ina seem pretty slim, and the chance that they'd both have a banana salad recipe worth copying a statistical impossibility. But there they are: Edith Terrill, Ruth Cutsinger, and Ina Brown.

Unlike the majority of my female friends, the ladies in Gran's circle seemed pretty fulfilled by the confines of home and hearth. None of these dames were going to write a novel or run for public office, but there are other ways to jockey for one's name to live beyond the tombstone. If I, the oldest grandchild, find myself in receipt of Cleda Lotsy's Broccoli–Lima Bean Casserole, Frances Combs's Congo Squares, Jo Riddell's Wet Cake, Ruth Hedrick's Cold Chicken Pie, and Ruth Sheeley's Shrimp Mousse, might not their descendants find themselves curators of my grandmother Elva Brockway's god-knows-what?

I have to tell you, I'm more than a little intrigued by that Broccoli–Lima Bean Casserole, which makes duplicate appearances, once credited to Cleda and once to someone named Janice. I wonder if disputed authorship led to a catfight. In high school, my friend Marybeth and I nearly came to blows over which of our mothers had invented Italian Zucchini Crescent Pie. According to the Pillsbury Bake-Off website, it was neither. There, credit is assigned to one Millicent Nathan, who apparently rode my mother's Zucchini Crescent Pie to victory in 1980. And wait a second, wasn't Cleda's daughter named Janice?

Like the Refrigerated Crescent Dinner Rolls of the 1980s' Bake-Off winner, the ingredients called for in many of Gran's recipes have turned her card file into a time capsule, though not exactly in the way I had envisioned. I had always classified her as a no-nonsense farm cook, but as all those canned "cream of" soups attest, she wasn't a purist. Like the Mennonite woman I recently observed reading *Real Simple* on a flight from JFK to Columbus, Ohio, she was receptive to trends and products that could be incorporated into her established lifestyle. She never went as far as Koogle, the wacky flavored peanut butter my mother promised to buy me if I returned from Gnaw Bone with all of my underpants, or Molly McButter, which required no refrigeration and could be sprinkled over everything from popcorn to mashed potatoes, but rest assured that whoever had the Cool Whip account knew how to pitch to Gran's demographic.

Back when I was in pigtails, this pushy character named Sarah Tucker used to come on at least once a commercial break to bray that Cool Whip was the only dessert topping she'd ever serve her guests at Tucker Inn, a tidy-looking Victorian with rocking chairs lining its front porch. Gran seemed to think Sarah Tucker was a real person, and spoke of her with all the fond familiarity she accorded Merv Griffin, Percy Faith, Andy Williams, and the ladies who shared her table at the Scottish Rite's monthly luncheons. Much as my refrigerator always contains two or three tubs of organic, nonfat plain yogurt, hers was kept loyally stocked with Sarah's beloved Cool Whip.

From time to time, I like to play this little parlor game wherein I list Gran's essential pantry items, and then compare them to my own. My "indispensable" column undergoes a major overhaul every few months or so, but hers remained remarkably steadfast. As of this writing, Gran's Campbell's cream of celery is my fish sauce. Her Crisco, my almond butter. For every top Gran popped off a can of Durkee french fried onions, I've soaked an ancho chili. Her greens came canned or frozen. Mine come in great, unwieldy bundles, difficult to cram into the vegetable bin, so sandy it's like they've got a second home in Montauk. I go through garlic in quantities sufficient to ward off legions of vampires. Hers, powdered, was entombed in a largely decorative spice rack. I keep my seasonings in old baby food and jelly jars, precariously stacked on an untidy glass shelf that also houses our sake cups, my paternal grandmother's sugar bowl, a rubber band ball I'm cultivating, and a shot glass featuring a character named Drinky Crow.

Gran's culinary trajectory, from cradle to grave, was as straight as an arrow's, but mine is all over the map, which is why I occasionally find myself unable to follow through on the dinner I have planned when it is discovered that once again, I have run out of some indispensable ingredient, like lemongrass or fresh ginger or mango powder or coriander or jalapeños.

*

Despite the cool culinary reception of my first ten years, I am a sucker for any story that goes into loving detail about the aroma of the sea bass Grandma steamed with black bean sauce every New Year's. I've got a near-insatiable hankering for anything in which Mama hauls home a big old plank of *bacala* in anticipation of *Natale* or squats on the floor to knead dough for *chappatis* or, alternatively, tortillas. Frequently, these sort of reminiscences come hitched to mea culpas for having let the desire to be like everyone else eclipse one's appreciation of an immigrant parent's decidedly non-American-seeming cuisine.

Wow, maybe Inky can grow up to write one of those, in which case, I hope her publisher won't care that the Old Country is Indiana. Judging by what I serve for dinner on any given night, they could be forgiven for thinking it's India, Mexico, or Japan. The kind of grub that Mama's Food Shop sells like hotcakes might not top my charts, but I'm happy to read about it. I know they didn't have much to eat in *The Grapes of Wrath*, but somehow between them, John Steinbeck and Ma Joad always managed to make it to sound pretty good. In fact, I wouldn't be surprised if Ma and Gran had some recipes in common. Not Mercedes Harris's Champagne Dessert, but maybe Hush Puppies or Kentucky Spoon Bread. Simple pleasures. "Hey, kids, did you know that when I was little, my grandmother and I used to make cookies for every holiday?" I ask.

"You've told us this before," Inky points out, but for her brother, still little enough to have zero memory of the kids he went to school with the year before last, this is hot news.

"We had cookie cutters shaped like pumpkins for Halloween or bunnies and eggs for Easter," I continue. "And if there was no holiday, that was okay, too, because we had one that was shaped like a maple leaf—"

"When is it going to be my birthday?" Milo breaks in with the solipsism of youth, something I assure you I know nothing about.

"July thirteenth," I shoot back, without breaking stride. "You know, my grandmother was the one who gave me that cookbook you guys have to be careful with, you know, the yellow one you ripped the cover off of when you were little. Yeah, I used to cook all sorts of things out of there when I was Inky's age."

"You used to like to cook?" Inky's ears prick up.

"I thought you said you'd heard all this."

"Just the part about the cookies."

"Oh, well, in that case, sure. I loved to cook. I cooked with Granny and my grandmother, whose name was Gran-Gran, and sometimes when I went to camp, I got to cook outdoors. And then when I got a bit older, I started cooking with my friends, and then I worked in a lot of restaurants and traveled around, eating the sorts of things you get to eat in other countries, and then I met your father and moved to New York and had you guys, and now I'm a big star on the Food Network."

"Nooo!" the children jeer, thrilled as ever to catch a glaring inconsistency in my narrative. Yeah, they nailed me all right. We don't even have cable.

"Eat that good rice pudding Mama made for us," Greg prompts automatically, noticing Inky's reluctance to bring her spoon anywhere near her mouth. "It's delicious."

Not to her, but that's okay. Courtesy bites are strictly optional when it comes to dessert, though I still wish she could draw on some inner reserves, push past the presence of the raisins, and try just a taste of this dish. Lord knows how many times it filled my 'zert hole up. It was never anything special, nothing you'd want to crown in Cool Whip in order to represent at bridge club or a family reunion. I mean, it takes all of five minutes' preparation before going into the oven and uses leftover rice. Discovering it in Gran's recipe box filled me with a sense of well-being, like the first few seconds of consciousness after a dream so real, you wake convinced that a long-gone loved one has been sitting on the edge of your bed.

ayun's gran's rice custard

Order Chinese carryout in such quantities that there's more rice than you can possibly eat.

The next day, preheat the oven to 350°.

Butter a baking dish, one of those big rectangular ones, or better yet, maybe 6 or so individual serving–sized Pyrex bowls like my grandmother had. (I guess you could call them ramekins, though Gran never would have.)

Beat 2 eggs in a mixing bowl.

Then add:

- ½ teaspoon of salt
- 1 teaspoon of vanilla
- 2 cups of milk
- ⅓ cup of sugar
- ½ cup of raisins
- 1 cup of that leftover rice

Dot with little shards of butter, sprinkle with cinnamon, and bake for 30 minutes, or until the custard sets.

acknowledgments

So many people have contributed to making me the bundle of contradictions or, as some would say, outright nightmare that I am today, I'm not quite sure where to start.

Thanks to my family. On the end that raised me, we have Betsy and Art Harris, Reed Halliday, and Bob Brockway, as well as my late grandmother, Elva Brockway. Currently putting up with me on a daily basis are Greg, India, and Milo Kotis. Heart-shaped waffles all around.

Thank you to Cynthia MacCollum and Lisa Hickey for both their friendship and their fine examples. Other culinarily gifted friends somehow managed to keep themselves out of these pages, among them Karen Christopher, Sarah Cooke, and Spencer Kayden. Oh, now wait, there's that part where I've got Spencer saying she's going to fuck up some baked beans. . . .

Sean Bosker not only encouraged me to write about my experience with listeria, he fired up my computer and banged out the first three paragraphs. I changed every word to avert a potential lawsuit, but still, thanks, Sean.

No matter how many cappuccinos I might buy, I'll remain deeply indebted to the staff of the Flying Saucer Café, particularly John Brien, Julie Ipcar, Carrie Ewers, and Matt Stefanik, who allowed me and my laptop to monopolize the table by the door for literally hours at a stretch. I think the record was six. Please patronize the Flying Saucer Café whenever you find yourself in Brooklyn!

And while you're at it, swing by Fish Tales to say hi to Alex and Louis, just like I'm doing here.

To the readers of the *East Village Inky,* I extend my undying gratitude *and* a big old coconut-flavored spanking. Promoting my career when you're supposed to be fixing dinner for your children? For shame!

I'd like to thank the Academy. When can I expect to receive my award?

There are so many bazillions of books out there, it always makes my day when an independent bookseller or reviewer or blogger sees fit to single out one of mine. In a positive way, I mean. The Amazon.com customer who gave me fewer stars than she gave the Deluxe Music Motion Mobile can kiss my ass, but everyone else gets five gold stars with my compliments.

Thanks to Brooke Warner, Krista Rafanello, Laura Mazer, and Dave "Fecal Soup" Awl for graciously permitting me to pepper them with all sorts of foolish book-related concerns.

Okay, here's who I really want to thank: my editor, Leslie Miller, and not just for letting me keep "bazillions" in the paragraph preceding this one. Actually, she's more of my coauthor, not to mention a dear and hilarious friend who once sent me a ten-pound *molcajete* for no apparent reason. I swear to god, I weighed the thing in my bathroom. Then I made guacamole.

index

n

o

p

q

r

s

t

u

v

w

y

z

about the author

ayun halliday is the sole staff member of the quarterly zine the *East Village Inky* and the author of *Job Hopper, No Touch Monkey!*, and *The Big Rumpus*. She is *BUST* magazine's "Mother Superior" columnist and also contributes to *Hip Mama, Bitch,* and more anthologies than you can shake a stick at without dangling a participle. She lives in a small apartment in Brooklyn with her husband and their two well-documented children.

Dare to be heinie. Visit www.ayunhalliday.com.

selected titles from seal press

For more than twenty-five years, Seal Press has published groundbreaking books. By women. For women. Visit our website at www.sealpress.com.

Job Hopper: The Checkered Career of a Down-Market Dilettante by Ayun Halliday. $14.95. 1-58005-130-8. Halliday, quickly becoming one of America's funniest writers, chronicles her hilarious misadventures in the working world.

No Touch Monkey! And Other Travel Lessons Learned Too Late by Ayun Halliday. $14.95. 1-58005-097-2. A self-admittedly bumbling vacationer, Halliday shares—with razor-sharp wit and to hilarious effect—the travel stories most are too self-conscious to tell.

The Big Rumpus: A Mother's Tale from the Trenches by Ayun Halliday. $15.95. 1-58005-071-9. Creator of the wildly popular zine *East Village Inky*, Halliday describes, in words and line drawings, the quirks and everyday travails of her young urban family, warts and all.

Confessions of a Naughty Mommy: How I Found My Lost Libido by Heidi Raykeil. $14.95. 1-58005-157-X. The Naughty Mommy shares her bedroom woes and woo-hoos with other mamas who are rediscovering their sex lives after baby and are ready to think about it, talk about it, and DO it.

The Unsavvy Traveler: Women's Comic Tales of Catastrophe edited by Rosemary Caperton, Anne Mathews, and Lucie Ocenas. $15.95. 1-58005-142-1. Thirty bitingly funny essays respond to the question: "What happens when trips go wrong?"

The Risks of Sunbathing Topless: And Other Funny Stories from the Road edited by Kate Chynoweth. $15.95. 1-58005-141-3. From Kandahar to Baja to Moscow, these wry, amusing essays capture the comic essence of bad travel, and the female experience on the road.